UNIVERSALLY CHALLENGED

UNIVERSALLY CHALLENGED

QUIZ CONTESTANTS SAY THE FUNNIEST THINGS

WENDY ROBY

MICHAEL O'MARA BOOKS

First published in Great Britain in 2010 by
Michael O'Mara Books Limited
9 Lion Yard
Tremadoc Road
London SW4 7NQ

Papers used by Michael O'Mara Books Limited are natural, recyclable products
made from wood grown in sustainable forests. The manufacturing processes
conform to the environmental regulations of the country of origin.

A CIP catalogue record for this book is available from the British Library.

ISBN: 978-1-84317-466-0

5 7 9 10 8 6

www.mombooks.com

Cover design by Ana Bjezancevic
Text design and typesetting by K DESIGN, Somerset
Illustrations by Andrew Pinder

Printed and bound in Great Britain by CPI Cox & Wyman, Reading, RG1 8EX

CONTENTS

Introduction 7

I've Only Seen the Film 9

Gastronomically Challenged 17

Strange Logic 26

Wheel of Misfortune 38

Nice Try 44

Facts and Figures 54

Bum Notes 62

Less Haste, More Speed 67

Withering Looks 75

Pass the Atlas, Dear 79

Cultural Insensitivity 89

Mishaps and Mishears 99

Animal Magic 102

Whole Lotta History 109

And the Oscar Goes to 118

The End of the Pier 126

Naughty by Nature 134

Bad Sports 140

Clues and Cheats 144

Random Revelations 158

Love and Marriage 175

Dumb and Dumber and Dumbererer 179

And Finally ... A Turkey 190

Acknowledgements 192

INTRODUCTION

Something strange – something slightly silly – happens to members of the public when they go on TV quiz shows. Wide-eyed and terrified as motorway rabbits, their minds have a tendency to go blank. And suddenly the answer to even the simplest, first-round-of-*Who-Wants-to-Be-a-Millionaire?*, 'What-colour-is-the-sun?'-style question eludes them.

Of course, everyone's general knowledge suffers from shaming gaps; it's just that they usually appear when you're at home, blissfully barking answers at the television while your partner scoffs along. The fact that you have managed to convince yourself that Jane Seymour can't have been a wife of Henry VIII because Jane Seymour is an actress on the popular television show *Dr Quinn: Medicine Woman* – well, that's fine, because *you're* not on the TV. No one's around to hear your stupid answers.

If we're honest, the rank stupidity of quiz contestants just makes us feel better about our own intellectual shortcomings. Personally, I experience a peculiar surge of pleasure when Jeremy Paxman screams 'Come OOOOOOOON!' at a particularly foppish Oxbridge oaf. But at least the questions on *University Challenge* are hard. Imagine being invited on to *Are You Smarter Than a 10 Year Old?* and coming up short. It doesn't bear thinking about.

Perhaps we watch these shows precisely *because* the answers are so gloriously brainless. If *Family Fortunes'* incredible run of thirty years tells us anything, it's this: never misunderestimacize the public. People are thicker than you think.

Now, *Encyclopaedia Britannica,* anyone?

> **For nerds, squares and boffins everywhere.**
> **Your time will come.**

I'VE ONLY SEEN
THE FILM

What's amazingly handy about those funny, old-fashioned rectangles with all the paper and words in them (you know, like the thing you've got in your hand right now), is that, if you read them, you tend to, well, *learn* stuff. Unfortunately, as this bewildering collection of literature-related wrongness demonstrates, there's no guarantee that any of this stuff will stick in your memory for very long. With so many books and plays to remember, confusing *Cat on a Hot Tin Roof* with *The Cat in the Hat*, or confidently declaring that Charlotte Brontë was a character in one of Jane Austen's novels, seems quite forgiveable ... Doesn't it?

● ●

From *Bingo America* (GSN):

Richard Karn: Asterix the Gaul fought which enemy?
Contestant: Klingons.

● ●

From *Brainteaser* (Channel Five):

Alex Lovell: Which literary hunchback lived in Notre-Dame
and fell in love with Esmeralda?
Contestant: Nostradamus.

From *Dale's Supermarket Sweep* (ITV):

Dale Winton: In Shakespeare's play *A Midsummer Night's Dream*, who was king of the fairies?

Contestant: I'm not very good at history.

From *Dog Eat Dog* (BBC):

Ulrika Jonsson: Shakespeare. In *A Midsummer Night's Dream*, which character assumed the head of an ass?

Contestant: Macbeth.

Ulrika Jonsson: Who wrote *The Lord of the Rings*?

Contestant: Enid Blyton.

Ulrika Jonsson: What distinguished prize did Albert Einstein win in 1921 for his work in physics?
Contestant: The Booker Prize.

From *Family Feud* (CBS):

Host: Name one of *The Three Bears*.
Contestant: Yogi?

> **Host:** Name an item of clothing worn by the Three Musketeers.
> **Contestant:** A horse.

From *Family Fortunes* (ITV):

Les Dennis: Name someone associated with Robinson Crusoe.
Contestant: Peter Pan.

From *National Lottery Jet Set* (BBC):

Eamonn Holmes: Complete the title of this Oliver Goldsmith novel, *The Vicar of* …?
Contestant: *Dibley*.

Eamonn Holmes: What year is the title of a famous novel by George Orwell?
Contestant: *1949*.

Eamonn Holmes: What's the name of the playwright commonly known by the initials GBS?
Contestant: William Shakespeare.

Eamonn Holmes: Who wrote *The Catcher in the Rye*?
Contestant: Chaucer.

From *Steve Wright in the Afternoon* (BBC Radio 2):

Steve Wright: Which legendary blood-sucking creature was created by Bram Stoker?
Contestant: The leech.

• •

From *Sale of the Century* (NBC):

Host: What do we call a Japanese poem of seventeen syllables
that almost always refers to a season of the year?
Contestant: Miyoshi Umeki.

• •

From *The Weakest Link* (BBC):

Anne Robinson: Which Roman poet wrote the *The Aeneid*:
Virgil or Brains?
Contestant: Brains.

Anne Robinson: Name a book written by Jane Austen.
Contestant: *Charlotte Brontë*.

Anne Robinson: Complete the title of the well-known play,
The Iceman ... what?
Contestant: *Melts*.

Anne Robinson: In modern literature, who wrote the novel
American Psycho?
Contestant: Barbara Cartland.

Anne Robinson: Complete the title of this novel by Henry
James: *The Turn of the* ... what?
Contestant: *Century*.

Anne Robinson: Iago and Desdemona are characters in which
Shakespeare play?
Contestant: I did English literature at university. Um ... *Hamlet*?

Anne Robinson: For which book did Salman Rushdie win the Booker prize?
Contestant: *The Wind in the Willows.*

Anne Robinson: Sancho Panza was the companion of which famous fictional character?
Contestant: Rupert Bear.

Anne Robinson: The action of which Shakespeare play takes place between dusk on January 5th and dawn on January 6th?
Contestant: *A Midsummer Night's Dream.*

Anne Robinson: The adjective 'Rubenesque', meaning a plump, voluptuous woman, is derived from the work of which seventeenth-century Flemish artist?
Contestant: Aretha Franklin.

Anne Robinson: What 'T' is a novel by Irvine Welsh featuring the characters Begbie, Renton and Sick Boy?
Contestant: *Treasure Island.*

Anne Robinson: The nineteenth-century novel by the Russian author Dostoevsky is *Crime and …* what?
Contestant: *Prejudice.*

Anne Robinson: Who wrote *Cat on a Hot Tin Roof?*
Contestant: Dr Seuss.

Anne Robinson: William Burroughs' novel, first published in 1959, was *The Naked* ... what?

Contestant: *Chef.*

Anne Robinson: In books that are written in English, each line is printed and read starting at which side of the page?

Contestant: The right.

Anne Robinson: What's the nationality of the philosopher Jean-Paul Sartre?

Contestant: Italian.

Anne Robinson: In Tolkien's *Lord of the Rings* trilogy, the third and final book is called *The Return of the* ... what?

Contestant: *Jedi.*

Anne Robinson: Can you complete the title of the book by Jerome K. Jerome, *Three Men in a* ...?

Contestant: *Baby.*

• •

From *Who Wants to Be a Millionaire?* (ITV):

Chris Tarrant: Which of these is the title of a Shakespeare play:
a) *As You Like It,* b) *As You Love It,* c) *As You Wish It* or
d) *As You Want It?*
Contestant: I don't know. Can I phone a friend?

• •

From LBC Radio:

Host: Which French author has been translated into more
languages than any other French author in the world?
Contestant: Chaucer.

• •

GASTRONOMICALLY CHALLENGED

Considering the modern obsession with cooking and the explosion of interest in all things organic, macrobiotic and otherwise untainted, it's rather refreshing that the People of Quiz remain largely unmoved by silly notions of food-based snobbery. That said, you could argue that the bizarre 'foods' our bewildered quiz contestants profess to enjoy have a Heston Blumenthal-like quality in their own right. And if he can build a career on bacon-and-egg-flavoured ice cream, who are we to say that spaghetti isn't an appropriate bathtime snack?

Now eat up, or there'll be nothing for afters.

• •

From *Bingo America* (GSN):

Richard Karn: Name one of Italy's most famous historic monuments.
Contestant: The Leaning Tower of Pizza.

Richard Karn: What is a mixture of avocado, chilli and lime juice commonly known as?
Contestant: Guatemala.

Richard Karn: What is both a Chinese appetizer and a traditional Easter event?
Contestant: Wonton dim sum?

Richard Karn: Which Joseph founded a famous chain of tea shops, the first one opening in London in 1894?
Contestant: Goebbels.

From *Family Feud* (CBS):

Host: Name one thing you put on a pizza.
Contestant: Rice.

Host: Name something you make out of flowers.
Contestant: Cookies.

Host: Name something you put cinnamon on.
Contestant: Butter.

Host: Name something you squeeze.
Contestant: Peanut butter?

Host: Name something you wouldn't want the police to find in the trunk of your car.
Contestant: Pickles.

Host: Name a farm animal that the farmer may grow so fond of, he might not want to eat it.
Contestant: Dog.

Host: Name a fast-food restaurant with somebody's first or last name in the title.
Contestant: Burger King.

Host: Name a food dieters dream about.
Contestant: Losing weight.

Host: Name a food people give as a gift.
Contestant: Lasagne.

Host: Name something besides jelly that comes in flavours.
Contestant: Jelly.

Host: Name something that comes in pairs.
Contestant: Bananas.

Host: The perfect dessert for a supermodel.
Contestant: Chocolate cake.
Contestant 2: Brownies.

Host: Name a job that helicopters are used for.
Contestant: Tuna fishing.

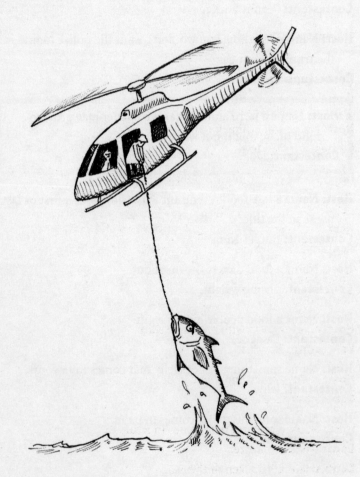

Host: Name something that doesn't work without water.
Contestant: Ice cream cone?

Host: Name something you eat too much of.
Contestant: Food?

> **Host:** Name a food that's difficult to eat if you wear false teeth.
> **Contestant:** Glue?

Host: Name something you put in empty coffee cans.
Contestant: Spaghetti.

Host: Name something you put in tea.
Contestant: Tea bag.

Host: Name something you rent for a party.
Contestant: Food?

Host: Name a food that makes noise when you eat it.
Contestant: A really loud hamburger?

Host: Name a food that's red on the inside.
Contestant: Kiwi.

Host: Name a food with an edible skin.
Contestant: Banana.

Host: Name something that can be smooth or bumpy.
Contestant: Bread.

Host: Name a seafood that comes in a can, besides tuna.
Contestant: Albacore.
Contestant 2: Chicken of the Sea.

Host: Name something that a child takes to the bathtub
with him.
Contestant: Spaghetti and meatballs?

Host: Name something in a candy bar, besides chocolate.
Contestant: Candy.

Host: Name something that uses microchips.
Contestant: Deep-fat fryer.

Host: Name something you can put hot tea into.
Contestant: Kettle.

Host: Name something you keep in a kitchen canister.
Contestant: Cans?

Host: Name something you keep in a kitchen container.
Contestant: Scotch.

Host: Name something Scotch.
Contestant: Water?

Host: Name something people buy to impress other people.
Contestant: Cookies.

Host: Name something that might be a pizza topping in a
horror movie.
Contestant: Faeces.

Host: Name a fruit used in pies.
Contestant: Squash?

Host: Name a fruit found in fruitcake.
Contestant: Booze?

Host: Name a kind of ache.
Contestant: Pancake.

From *Family Fortunes* (ITV):

Les Dennis: Name a kind of ache.
Contestant: Filet-O-Fish. [Did the contestant hear 'hake'?!]

Les Dennis: What is the term for a female peacock?
Contestant: Turkey.

Les Dennis: Name a food people put ketchup on.
Contestant: Peas.

Les Dennis: Name a food that can be easily eaten without chewing.
Contestant: Chips?

Les Dennis: Name something people eat with steak.
Contestant: Kidney pie?

From *Fifteen to One* (Channel 4):

William G. Stewart: Which cathedral town on the River Severn shares its name with the sauce used in a Bloody Mary?
Contestant: Tomato.

From *Steve Wright in the Afternoon* (BBC Radio 2):

Steve Wright: What is the Italian word for 'motorway'?
Contestant: *Expresso.*

Steve Wright: What kind of creature is a kiwi?
Contestant: A fruit.

From *The Weakest Link* (BBC):

Anne Robinson: Which beverage has varieties including latte and mocha?
Contestant: Milk.

Anne Robinson: What 'C' is a wine drunk on special occasions?
Contestant: Chardonnay.

Anne Robinson: What fruit is used to produce the spirit brandy?
Contestant: Coconut.

Anne Robinson: Which hot drink is 'eat' an anagram of?
Contestant: Hot chocolate?

> **Anne Robinson:** Which product had an advertising ban
> imposed on it in 1999?
> **Contestant:** Marmalade.

From *The Weakest Link* (NBC):

Anne Robinson: There are three states of matter: solid, liquid
and … what?
Contestant: Jelly?

Anne Robinson: What 'G' is a brand of animal-shaped cheddar
crackers introduced by Pepperidge Farm in 1962?
Contestant: Oreos.

Anne Robinson: What hard cheese derives its name from the
city of Rome?
Contestant: Swiss.

Anne Robinson: Which Cluedo character has a military rank?
Contestant: Colonel Sanders.

STRANGE LOGIC

You may think that there are only right or wrong answers. Naturally, the point-scorers on quiz shows would agree with you – they insist on absolute accuracy: facts, figures and provable knowledge. But sometimes, when contestants fail to deliver the exact answer, there's a strange sort of *rightness* to their wrongness. In this topsy-turvy world, the worst answers become the best answers – even if they do display a spectacular disregard for common sense.

• •

From *Bingo America* (GSN):

Richard Karn: What's the fastest-selling drug?
Contestant: Marijuana/Vicodin.

• •

From *Family Feud* (CBS):

Host: Name a bird with a long neck.
Contestant: Naomi Campbell.

Host: Name an animal that's hard to tell what sex it is.
Contestant: An elephant.

Host: Name a month that's also a person's name.
Contestant: January.

Host: Name a pie that does not contain fruit.
Contestant: Lemon meringue.

Host: Name something made of wool.
Contestant: Sheep.

Host: Name a reason for standing up quickly.
Contestant: Being in church.

Host: Name a road sign that describes your love life.
Contestant: Do Not Enter.

Host: Name a slang name for 'policeman'.
Contestant: Dick.

Host: Name a slang word for 'man'.
Contestant: Homeboy.

Host: Name a question, such as 'How old are you?', that you might answer with a lie.
Contestant: 'Are you eighteen?'
Contestant 2: 'Are you fifty?'
Contestant 3: 'Are you thirty-nine?'

Host: Name an occupation where you might need a torch.
Contestant: A burglar.

Host: Name a specific place where you'd hate to be during a major power failure.
Contestant: In a car.

Host: Name a sport in which two people compete against each other.
Contestant: Checkers.

Host: Name a sport people play by themselves.
Contestant: Video games.

Host: Name a subject elderly people spend a lot of time discussing.
Contestant: Bingo.

Host: Name a sure cure for a hangover.
Contestant: Making love.

Host: Name a tall tourist attraction.
Contestant: Disneyland.

Host: Name a time when people go to bed.
Contestant: Night.

Host: Name a time when people wake up.
Contestant: Morning.

Host: Name a type of foreign money.
Contestant: Monopoly.

Host: Name an occupation requiring a college degree.
Contestant: Vice-president.

Host: Name something a girl should know about a man before she marries him.
Contestant: His name.

Host: Name something a hostess does to let her guests know it's time to leave.
Contestant: Goes to bed.

Host: Name something a husband and wife should have separately.
Contestant: Parents.

Host: Name something a woman out on a date would hate to discover on her face.
Contestant: A bogey.

Host: Name something an airline passenger might be holding during a bumpy flight.
Contestant: A lucky rabbit's foot.

Host: Name something an elephant has that's huge.
Contestant: Butt.

Host: Name something that makes you feel uneasy all day long
if you forget to do it in the morning.
Contestant: Get dressed.

Host: Name something associated with Cuba.
Contestant: It's in South America.

Host: Name something associated with *The X-Files*.
Contestant: Television.

Host: Name something dogs can do better than people.
Contestant: Pee.

> **Host:** Name something easy to do forwards, but difficult to do backwards.
> **Contestant:** Eating.

Host: Name something men do when they run out of clean underwear.

Contestant: Turn them inside out.

Host: Name something you buy in a larger size if you have a large family.

Contestant: Jeans.

Host: Name something you wish you had one of for each person in your home.

Contestant: A house.

Host: Name something you write on a holiday postcard.

Contestant: 'I'm going to send you a postcard home.'

Host: Name a reason for kneeling.

Contestant: To be beheaded.

Host: Name a place where you might see a whole lot of shaking going on.

Contestant: The malted milk factory.

Host: Name a place where you'd keep a pen.

Contestant: The zoo.

Host: Name a hobby people take up for the thrills involved.

Contestant: Stamp collecting.

Host: Name a famous Frank.

Contestant: French Franc?

Host: Name a kind of bank that doesn't deal with money.

Contestant: Sperm.

Host: Name something babies throw out of their crib.

Contestant: Prayer book.

Host: Name a kind of place where it's smart to know where the exits are.

Contestant: Church.

Host: Name a letter many words begin with.

Contestant: 'Dear John.'

Host: Name a measurement of time.

Contestant: Watch.

Host: Name an activity that is both healthy and fun.

Contestant: Sex.

Host: Name an occupation whose members must get tired of smiling.

Contestant: Game show host.

Host: Name a sport which would be hazardous in a nudist colony.

Contestant: Leapfrog.

Host: Name something specific kids leave behind when they move out of the house.

Contestant: Their parents/A blender/Boyfriend or girlfriend.

> **Host:** Name something that can kill a lively party.
> **Contestant:** A gun.

Host: Name something that comes in twelves.

Contestant: Dozens.

Host: Name something that dries up as it gets old.

Contestant: Water.

Host: Name something that's murder to clean up when you spill it.

Contestant: Blood.

Host: Name something with a hole in the middle.

Contestant: Hole punch.

Host: Name something a caveman would put on his to-do list.

Contestant: Buy a car.

Host: Name something you wear for protection.

Contestant: Gun.

> **Host:** Name something that falls from the trees.
> **Contestant:** A noisy bird.

Host: The section of the newspaper in which you'd be shocked to find your name.

Contestant: Weddings/Lost and Found.

Host: Another word for 'sleep'.
Contestant: 'Sleeping'/'A coma'.

Host: Someone Bugs Bunny might invite to his birthday party.
Contestant: Doc.

Host: Someone you'd never want to see the results of your IQ test.
Contestant: The IRS.

Host: Like 'sugar bowl', a bowl that's named for the substance it contains.
Contestant: Toilet bowl.

Host: Name something office workers turn off at the end of the day.
Contestant: Their brains.

> **Host:** Name a real person who made a living scaring people.
> **Contestant:** George Bush.

Host: Name something you see along the side of a street.
Contestant: Carnage.

Host: Name something people are careful to step over when they're walking.
Contestant: Spit.

Host: Name something people hold still for.
Contestant: When they have to go to the bathroom.

Host: The worst place to be when you need to use the restroom.
Contestant: On a game show.

• •

From *Family Fortunes* (ITV):

Les Dennis: Name a part of the body that can be flat.
Contestant: Head.

Les Dennis: Name a foreign country where it would be easy to
  put on weight.
Contestant: Paris.

Les Dennis: Name a kind of ache.
Contestant: Face-ache.

Les Dennis: Name a TV soap.
Contestant: Dove.

Les Dennis: Name something a car can have two of.
Contestant: Wheels.

Les Dennis: Name something people might be allergic to.
Contestant: Skiing.

Les Dennis: Name something slippery.
Contestant: A conman.

Les Dennis: Name something you see at every football game.
Contestant: Pies.

> **Les Dennis:** Name something you put on walls.
> **Contestant:** A roof.

Les Dennis: Name something you stroke.
Contestant: A match.

Les Dennis: Name something you throw away daily.
Contestant: Toilet paper.

Les Dennis: Name a polite word you'd use to swear.
Contestant: 'Bugger'.

Les Dennis: Name something you do in an anorak.
Contestant: Wear it.

From *Press Your Luck* (CBS):

Peter Tomarken: Part of a Christmas turkey.
Contestant: Stuffing.

From *Sale of the Century* (ITV):

Host: Finish the phrase 'Full of …' what?
Contestant: 'Crap'?

From *The Weakest Link* (BBC):

Anne Robinson: In government organizations, what does the letter 'M' stand for in MI5 and MI6?
Contestant: Murder.

Anne Robinson: 'No *what*, please; we're British'?
Contestant: 'Thank you'.

Anne Robinson: Oscar Wilde, Adolf Hitler and Jeffrey Archer have all written books about their experiences in what: prison, or the Conservative Party?
Contestant: The Conservative Party.

From *The Weakest Link* (NBC):

Anne Robinson: The law of what organization states that its members are 'brave, clean and reverent'?
Contestant: Alcoholics Anonymous.
[Real answer: the Boy Scouts.]

WHEEL OF MISFORTUNE

On *Wheel of Fortune* (ITV), contestants are pitted against each other to identify famous phrases, people and places. And perhaps this competitive element explains why their guesses are so desperately bad, even when the answers are spectacularly commonplace. Unless, of course, you really have heard the famous phrases 'self potato' and 'barbeque shit'.

Sadly, what follows can only be described as drawing a blank ...

Puzzle: At Sir Irving's knighting, the queen slipped with her sword. So instead of being knighted, Sir Irving was [what]ed?
Contestant's answer: Bar-mitzvahed?

Puzzle: S _ L F / P O _ T _ _ _ T
Contestant's answer: Self potato?
Answer: Self portrait.

Puzzle: _ / _ R _ _ P / _ _ / _ _ L L - _ _ S H _ R S
Contestant's answer: A group of pill-pushers?
Answer: A group of well-wishers.

Puzzle: B A R B E Q U E / S _ I T
Contestant's answer: Barbeque shit?
Answer: Barbeque spit.

Puzzle: _ I S H / L _ _ _
Contestant's answer: Fish love?
Answer: Wish list.

Puzzle: S T _ R _ F _ _ M / _ _ _
Contestant's answer: Styrofoam hat?
Answer: Styrofoam cup.

Puzzle: _ _ L L / T H E / _ M P _ R E
Contestant's answer: Lill the Vampire?
Answer: Kill the empire.

Puzzle: L _ T E - N I _ _ T / I N _ _ M E R _ I _ L S
Contestant's answer: Late-night intramuralist?
Answer: Late-night infomercials.

Puzzle: L A U N D R Y / _ _ _ T E
Contestant's answer: Laundry paste?
Answer: Laundry chute.

Puzzle: L _ S T / M _ _ _ T E / _ _ _ A I L S
Contestant's answer: Last minute cocktails?
Answer: Last minute details.

Puzzle: _ T / T A K E S / O N E / T O / K N O W / O N E
Contestant's answer: E.T. takes one to know one?
Answer: It takes one to know one.

Puzzle: K I _ _ / I T / A N D / M A K _ / I T / B _ T T _ R
Contestant's answer: Kick it and make it better?
Answer: Kiss it and make it better.

Puzzle: T E N - G A L L O N / _ A T
Contestant's answer: Ten-gallon cat?
Answer: Ten-gallon hat.

Puzzle: L _ T T E R _ / T _ _ _ E T
Contestant's answer: Lottery toilet?
Answer: Lottery ticket.

Puzzle: _ I N _ E R S / A N D / _ O E S
Contestant's answer: Miners and hoes?
Answer: Fingers and toes.

Puzzle: _ _ _ D / B _ R N _ N G / S T _ V E
Contestant's answer: Food burning stove?
Answer: Wood burning stove.

Puzzle: _ N / _ C _ / O _ / K I _ D N E _ S
Contestant's answer: An ace of kidneys?
Answer: An act of kindness.

Puzzle: _ _ S T A R D - F I L L E D / _ H _ _ _ L A T E /
  E _ L A I R
Contestant's answer: Mustard-filled chocolate eclair?
Answer: Custard-filled chocolate eclair.

Puzzle: _ I L D / _ I N _ O
Contestant's answer: Wild bingo?
Answer: Wild dingo.

Puzzle: A N / _ _ _ Y / C H I L D
Contestant's answer: An ugly child?
Answer: An only child.

Puzzle: _ T / _ _ / _ _ T ' S / E N _
Contestant's answer: At my cat's end?
Answer: At my wit's end.

Puzzle: S L E E _ I N G / _ _ _ _ _ Y
Contestant's answer: Sleeping dopey?
Answer: Sleeping beauty.

Puzzle: Y O U R / _ O O S E / I S / C O O K E D
Contestant's answer: Your moose is cooked?
Answer: Your goose is cooked.

Puzzle: C O _ _ E R / B A R B E R _ H O P
Contestant's answer: Copper barbershop?
Contestant 2's answer: Quarter barbershop?
Answer: Corner barbershop.

Puzzle: S T R A W _ _ R _ Y / L _ P / G _ _ _ S
Contestant's answer: Strawberry lip girls.
Answer: Strawberry lip gloss.

Puzzle: A L L / Y _ U / C A N / E A T / T A C _ / B A R
Contestant's answer: All you can eat take bar?
Answer: All you can eat taco bar.

Puzzle: _ N L _ _ D _ N G / T H E / D _ S H _ _ S H E R
Contestant's answer: Emptying the dishwasher.
Answer: Unloading the dishwasher.

Puzzle: S P A M / F I L _ E R
Contestant's answer: Spam filler.
Answer: Spam filter.

Puzzle: G R _ S S - R O O T S / M O _ _ M _ N T
Contestant's answer: Grass-roots monument?
Answer: Grass-roots movement.

Puzzle: S H _ P P _ N G / _ _ S T
Contestant's answer: Shopping post?
Answer: Shopping list.

Puzzle: G I V E N / H A L _ / A / C H A N C E
Contestant's answer: Is the missing letter a 'P'?
Answer: Given half a chance.

Puzzle: G L E A _ I N G / W H I T E / S A N D / B E A C H
Contestant's answer: Is the missing letter a 'D'?
Answer: Gleaming white sand beach.

NICE TRY

When in doubt, lark about. What follows are answers that – though wrong – have a certain daft élan about them. It's tempting to imagine that these particular contestants were joking all along: they weren't bothered about winning the speedboat, caravan or dishwasher; they just wanted to be on the TV so that they could tell all their friends. This species of cheeky contestant doesn't know much – and isn't going to waste time trying.

So, your starter for ten is to name Madonna's 1990 sell-out tour. Just a hint: it's not *Blonde Tart*.

• •

From *Are You Smarter Than a 10 Year Old?* (SKY1):

Noel Edmonds: Was the Tyrannosaurus Rex a carnivore or a herbivore?
Contestant: No, it was a dinosaur.

• •

From *Beat the Nation* (Channel 4):

Tim Brooke-Taylor: The Ashmolean in Oxford was England's first what?
Contestant: Indian restaurant.

From *The Big Quiz* (LBC Radio):

Gary King: Name the funny men who once entertained kings
and queens at court.
Contestant: Lepers.

• •

From *Blockbusters* (ITV):

Bob Holness: What 'E' is the world's highest mountain?
Contestant: Everglades.

Bob Holness: What 'W' is Ronald Reagan's middle name?
Contestant: We-publican.

• •

From *Family Feud* (CBS):

Host: Name a famous Arnold.
Contestant: Arthur Miller.

Host: Name a song with the word 'moon' in the title.
Contestant: 'Blue Suede Moon'.

Host: Name a song with the word 'yellow' in the title.
Contestant: 'Yellow Garden'.

Host: Name a tradition associated with Christmas.
Contestant: Hanukkah.

Host: Name an astronaut.
Contestant: Neil Young.

Host: Name a brand of gasoline.
Contestant: Regular?
Contestant 2: Unleaded?
Contestant 3: Ethyl?

Host: Name a famous Peter.
Contestant: Peter.

Host: Name an attraction you see in every parade.
Contestant: Bearded lady.

Host: Name something that rhymes with 'coke'.
Contestant: 'Toke'?

Host: Name something you do before going to bed.
Contestant: Sleep.

Host: Name one of Santa's reindeer.
Contestant: Nixon.

Host: Name one of the Seven Dwarves.
Contestant: Snoopy.

> **Host:** Name something you know about Rudy Giuliani.
> **Contestant:** Absolutely nothing.

Host: Name the movie where John Travolta gave his most memorable performance.
Contestant: *The John Travolta Biography*.

Host: Name a real or fictional famous Willie.
Contestant: Willie-the-Pooh.

Host: Name a famous Hogan.
Contestant: The Hogan.

• •

From *This Morning with Richard and Judy* (ITV):

Fern Britton: If you're claustrophobic, what are you traditionally afraid of?

Contestant: Open spaces.

• •

Judy Finnigan: What were the gifts the Three Wise Men brought to the Baby Jesus?

Contestant: Gold, platinum and silver.

. . . .

From *Family Fortunes* (ITV):

Les Dennis: Name a famous Royal.
Contestant: Mail.

Les Dennis: Name a famous Scotsman.
Contestant: Jock.

> **Les Dennis:** Name something you wear on a beach.
> **Contestant:** A deckchair.

. . . .

From *Fifteen to One* (Channel 4):

William G. Stewart: In the novel and film, what is *Howard's End*?
Contestant: A boatyard.

William G. Stewart: Which mobile phone company has the slogan 'The future's bright, the future's Orange'?
Contestant: Virgin.

. . . .

From *National Lottery Jet Set* (BBC):

Eamonn Holmes: Which chapel ceiling did Michelangelo famously paint?
Contestant: The Sixteenth Chapel.

. . . .

From *The Richard Allinson Show* (BBC Radio 2):

Richard Allinson: What international brand shares its name with the Greek goddess of victory?
Contestant: [after long deliberation] Kellogg's?

• •

From *The Sara Cox Show* (BBC Radio 1):

Sara Cox: 'Beauty is in the eye of the …' what?
Contestant: 'Tiger'.

• •

From *Steve Wright in the Afternoon* (BBC Radio 2):

Steve Wright: What do you call the indigenous people of
Australia?
Contestant: Australians.

• •

From *The Weakest Link* (BBC):

Anne Robinson: What 'A' is the term for a set of symbols in
which each character represents a simple speech sound?
Contestant: Aural.

Anne Robinson: In traffic, what 'J' is where two roads meet?
Contestant: Jool carriageway.

> **Anne Robinson:** What was the name of Madonna's concert
> tour in 1990?
> **Contestant:** *Blonde Tart.*

Anne Robinson: Which actress named Patricia is the wife of
Nicolas Cage?
Contestant: Patricia Routledge.

Anne Robinson: Which 'B' completes the title of the book by
Lord Baden-Powell: *Scouting for …* what?
Contestant: *Business.*

Anne Robinson: The Bible: The New Testament. The Four Gospels were written by Matthew, Mark, Luke and …?

Contestant: [long pause] Joe?

Anne Robinson: In what European country was actor Antonio Banderas born?

Contestant: Mexico.

Anne Robinson: Space exploration. What does the acronym NASA stand for?

Contestant: National Socialist Space Satellite.

Anne Robinson: In agriculture, irrigation involves supplying farmland with which substance essential for growth?

Contestant: Weeds.

Anne Robinson: Which Roman statesman gave his name to the month of July?

Contestant: Augustus.

Anne Robinson: What man-made structure built during the third century BC is often said to be visible from space?

Contestant: The Millennium Dome.

From *The Weakest Link* (**NBC**):

Anne Robinson: The Sea-Tac Airport in Washington is named after the city of Seattle and what other city?

Contestant: Washington.

Anne Robinson: What name is given to the field of medicine that concerns the health of women?

Contestant: Womenology.

Anne Robinson: What stock symbol does International Business Machines trade under?

Contestant: NYB.

Anne Robinson: What computer company's name is abbreviated IBM?

Contestant: Apple.

Anne Robinson: What cast member of *The Carol Burnett Show* played the title character on NBC's *Mama's Family*?

Contestant: Mama.

Anne Robinson: Who are the cartoon mascots of Rice Krispies cereal?
Contestant: Crispy and Crunch.

From *The Vault* (ITV):

Host: In the Bible, which disciple betrayed Jesus?
Contestant: Solomon.

Host: Who recently celebrated their twenty-fifth anniversary of becoming prime minister of Britain?
Contestant: Tony Blair.

> **Host:** What is the name given to the condition where the sufferer can fall asleep at any time?
> **Contestant:** Nostalgia.

From GWR FM Bristol:

Host: What happened in Dallas on November 22, 1963?
Contestant: I don't know, I wasn't watching it then.

From Magic FM:

Host: What was the name of Tony Blair's chief spin-doctor who resigned last year?
Contestant: Iain Duncan Smith.

FACTS AND FIGURES

Contestants who get basic general knowledge questions wrong tend to get rather short shrift. 'What a moron!' you yell unforgivingly at the TV, forgetting for a moment that you, too, have no idea which continent Russia belongs to.

But wrong answers involving maths and science may find themselves getting slightly, er, taller shrift, as they're arguably the trickiest of game show subjects. Not least on *University Challenge*, where scientific questions get dragged out into novel-length monologues, sub-clause after sub-clause. So it seems churlish to blame those brainy undergrads for being the tiniest bit glassy-eyed by the time Jeremy Paxman gets to the question mark. And when he scoffs loudly as they fail to identify 'what number in decimal notation can be written in octal as 111' (??), it's hard not to feel sympathetic. Even if the brainboxes *could* confer, it wouldn't make any difference; they could be reading for a Ph.D. in the Applied Combinatorics of Discrete Mathematics (no, me neither) and still get a big fat fail.

But not *all* maths and science questions are difficult, as you shall soon see ...

• •

From *The Big Quiz* (LBC Radio):

Host: What is the largest carnivore that lives on the land?
Contestant: A whale.

• •

From *Bingo America* (GSN):

Richard Karn: How much does an ounce of gold weigh?
Contestant: Fourteen ounces.

• •

From *Blockbusters* (ITV):

Bob Holness: What 'O' is the generic term for any living animal
or plant, including bacteria and viruses?
Contestant: Orgasm.

Bob Holness: What 'S' is the nearest star to the earth?
Contestant: Saturn.

From *The Breakfast Show* (Wave FM):

Steve Powers: What does a planet orbit around?
Contestant: The galaxy? Or the moon?

From *Cash Cab* (ITV):

John Moody: In botany, what is the scientific term for a plant
that lives for more than two years?
Contestant: A tree.

From *Dog Eat Dog* (BBC):

Ulrika Jonsson: How many metres are there in a kilometre?
Contestant: Three.

> **Ulrika Jonsson:** If I travel at sixty miles an hour, how far
> do I travel in ten minutes?
> **Contestant:** Two hundred thousand miles.

From *Family Feud* (CBS):

Host: Name an invention that has replaced stairs.
Contestant: Wheel.

Host: Name something that is transplanted.
Contestant: Brain.

From *National Lottery Jet Set* (BBC):

Eamonn Holmes: What was invented in 1926 by John Logie Baird?
Contestant: Electricity.

From *Press Your Luck* (CBS):

Peter Tomarken: What eye ailment is the more common name for 'myopia'?
Contestant: Is it when you think you're always right?

From *Pyramid* (CBS):

Dick Clark: Ten times a hundred is what?
Contestant: A hundred?

From *Quiz Night* (BBC Radio Lancashire):

Host: Who discovered gravity when an apple fell from a tree and landed on his head?
Contestant: William Tell.

From *This Morning with Richard and Judy* (ITV):

Judy Finnigan: How many minutes are there in three-quarters of an hour?
Contestant: Sixty.

Richard Madeley: What planet is named after the goddess of love?
Contestant: Neptune.

From *The Weakest Link* (NBC):

Anne Robinson: What 'H' is the general term for a six-sided two-dimensional shape?
Contestant: Trapezoid.

Anne Robinson: What 'F' are ice crystals formed by condensation on surfaces below freezing?
Contestant: Icicles.

Anne Robinson: What is the largest planet visible from earth?
Contestant: The moon.

Anne Robinson: What is the name of the cord cut after a woman gives birth?
Contestant: Biblical cord.

From *The Weakest Link* (BBC):

Anne Robinson: What characterizes an amphibian?
Contestant: They can walk on land and water.

Anne Robinson: Cro-Magnon was an early form of which mammal, which now numbers in the millions?

Contestant: Crabs.

Anne Robinson: How many units are there in a dozen?

Contestant: Thirteen.

Anne Robinson: In human anatomy, the umbilicus is a scar in the centre of the abdomen that is more commonly known by what five-letter name?

Contestant: Button.

Anne Robinson: In maths, what is one half as a decimal?

Contestant: A quarter.

Anne Robinson: In science, what is botany the study of?

Contestant: Bottoms.

Anne Robinson: In medicine, what word beginning with 'G' represents the area of medicine specializing in the treatment of the elderly?

Contestant: Gynaecology.

Anne Robinson: In solid geometry, what 'H' is the name given to half a sphere?

Contestant: Half a circle.

Anne Robinson: In science, what was the surname of the German physicist who is credited with the invention of the mercury thermometer?

Contestant: Mercury.

Anne Robinson: The equator divides the world into how many hemispheres?

Contestant: Three.

Anne Robinson: What force of nature is responsible for keeping the earth, planets and asteroids in orbit around the sun?

Contestant: Delta Force.

Anne Robinson: What is the highest prime number under ten?

Contestant: Eleven.

Anne Robinson: What is the only even prime number?

Contestant: Nine.

Anne Robinson: What part of the human body is closest to the floor when we are walking?
Contestant: The head.

Anne Robinson: Which illness is named after its high temperature and red skin colouration?
Contestant: Yellow fever.

Anne Robinson: Which organ of the human body is used for smelling and breathing?
Contestant: The lungs.

Anne Robinson: In human development, what 'B' is the usual four-letter word for a newborn infant?
Contestant: Wasp.

BUM NOTES

It takes a certain sort of dedicated geek to remain *fully* engaged with the pop charts, especially when you've outgrown having posters on your wall. Far easier to admit defeat, or moan that it's all TOO LOUD and you 'can't hear the words properly'. On the other hand, with the music industry thriving thanks to cheap downloads and a bewildering plethora of TV talent shows, it's almost impossible to remain *completely* clueless.

So how to explain the discordant cacophony that follows? Fair enough, you might never have touched the cool brass of a trombone bell. Granted, you never actually learned to play the darned thing at school. But you know what it looks like, right? The one with the slidey thing? Oh. Apparently not.

• •

From *24 Hour Quiz* (ITV):

Shaun Williamson: Who sang the song 'Je t'aime' with Jane Birkin?
Contestant: Jacques Chirac?

• •

From *Bingo America* (GSN):

Richard Karn: Beethoven was the first composer to use what sliding brass instrument in a symphony?
Contestant: Violin.

From *Dog Eat Dog* (BBC):

Ulrika Jonsson: In what century was the composer J. S. Bach born?
Contestant: The twentieth century.

From *Family Feud* (CBS):

Host: Name a place you go to, to listen to music.
Contestant: iPod.

Host: Name an instrument in a country band?
Contestant: Cello.

From *The Ken Bruce Show* (BBC Radio 2):

Ken Bruce: Listen to the following piece of music and tell me
the name of the film adapted from a George Orwell novel
it featured in.
Contestant: *1989*?

From *National Lottery Jet Set* (BBC):

Eamonn Holmes: Dizzy Gillespie is famous for playing what?
Contestant: Basketball.

From *Steve Wright in the Afternoon* (BBC Radio 2):

Steve Wright: Who wrote the music for *Moon River* and
The Pink Panther?
Contestant: Mendelssohn.

From *The Weakest Link* (BBC):

Anne Robinson: Complete the title of this Destiny's Child song: 'Bills, Bills, ...' what?
Contestant: Don't know.

Anne Robinson: The song by Elvis that, on its reissue in 2005, became the 1000th number-one single in UK chart history is entitled 'One ...' what?
Contestant: 'A Little Less Conversation'.

Anne Robinson: In 1987, the Bangles had a number one UK hit with the song 'Walk Like an ...' what?
Contestant: 'Stranger'.

Anne Robinson: In an orchestra, the leader normally plays which instrument?
Contestant: The triangle.

Anne Robinson: In his 1961 number-one UK single 'Wooden Heart', Elvis sings in English and which other European language?
Contestant: English.

Anne Robinson: In music, what was the first name of the German composer Bach, who was born in 1685?
Contestant: Edward.

Anne Robinson: What is *divertimento*: an Italian road sign or a piece of music?
Contestant: An Italian road sign?

Anne Robinson: 'The Hallelujah Chorus' appears in which oratorio by Handel?
Contestant: *The Sound of Music.*

Anne Robinson: What was the nationality of the composer Sir Edward Elgar?
Contestant: Norwegian.

Anne Robinson: Which British composer took the music for 'Land of Hope and Glory' from his 'Pomp and Circumstance Marches'?
Contestant: Tchaikovsky.

Anne Robinson: Which musician famous for playing the piano honky-tonk-style died in the year 2000?
Contestant: Elton John.

> **Anne Robinson:** Which composer wrote *The Magic Flute*?
> **Contestant:** Bikini.

Anne Robinson: Which pop group, who once made a record with footballer Paul Gascoigne, took their name from an island off the coast of Northumberland?
Contestant: Gerry and the Pacemakers.

From BBC Radio Nottingham:

Host: Which classical composer became deaf in later life: Ludwig van …?
Contestant: [quick as a flash] Van Gogh.

From Q103 Cambridge:

Host: How many members were there of the boy band Five?
Contestant: Four.

LESS HASTE,
MORE SPEED

It's easy to see how some quiz show contestants might become a little bit overwhelmed under the glare of bright lights and multiple TV cameras. And how, when a whole set of shiny steak knives – or indeed, a shiny new speedboat – is revolving on the glittering prize carousel as a sequined lovely fans her hands about it, one might be tempted to answer as fast as is humanly possible.

The trouble is that these hasty answers often come out a bit, well, wrong – as if Joe Public has heard *a* question, but not necessarily *the* question being asked. And of course, this makes for some of the silliest answers you ever did hear.

• •

From *Family Feud* (CBS):

Host: Name a movie with the word 'King' in it.
Contestant: *King Dracula.*

Host: Name a reason you might stay inside on a beautiful day.
Contestant: It's raining.

Host: Name a sign of the Zodiac.
Contestant: April.

Host: Name a singer who is known by one name.
Contestant: Michael Jackson.

Host: Name a thing or place dogs are known to drink from.
Contestant: A hydrant.

> **Host:** Name a man's name that starts with the letter 'P'.
> **Contestant:** Porcupine.

Host: Name a three-letter word children first learn to spell.
Contestant: Daddy.

Host: Name a type of fruit found in tarts.
Contestant: Sweet tarts.

Host: Name a type of record.
Contestant: Floppy disk.

Host: Name a way parents reward children.
Contestant: Time out.

Host: Name a way you would treat a pet like a human.
Contestant: Take it to the vet.

Host: Name a weapon in the board game Clue.
Contestant: The dice.

Host: Name a word or phrase you hear in a tennis game.
Contestant: 'Fore.'

Host: Name an electric appliance designed to be handheld.
Contestant: Dishwasher.

Host: Name an ingredient you use to stuff chicken.
Contestant: Chicken.

Host: Name an occupation considered to be un-masculine.
Contestant: Truck driver.

Host: Name something associated with the Three Bears.
Contestant: Red Riding Hood.

Host: Name something in the garden that's green.
Contestant: The shed.

Host: Name a day of the year when you want to be with friends.
Contestant: December.

Host: Name a famous group of singers.
Contestant: The Simpsons.

Host: Name something made of leather that a cowboy uses.
Contestant: Purse.

Host: Name an instrument used by a doctor.
Contestant: Violin.

Host: Name a famous rock band that starts with the word 'the'.
Contestant: The Kiss.

Host: Name a farm animal that people have as a pet.
Contestant: Turkey.

Host: Name a food that comes smoked.
Contestant: Tobacco.

Host: Name a game played on a table besides cards.
Contestant: Poker.

Host: Name a holiday named after a person.
Contestant: January/Easter.

Host: Name a job around the house that has to be done every fall.
Contestant: Spring cleaning.

Host: Name a month of spring.
Contestant: Summer.

Host: Name an article of clothing kids usually don't like wearing.
Contestant: Gap.

Host: Name a drink you recognize by its smell.
Contestant: Potatoes.

Host: Name something you bang when it's not working right.
Contestant: Wall.

Host: Name something that you buy and then have to take good care of.
Contestant: An infant.

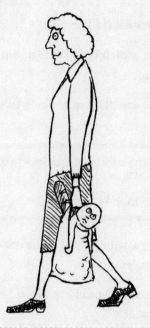

Host: The most famous Disney character, other than Mickey Mouse.
Contestant: Mighty Mouse?

Host: Besides a house or a car, the most expensive item you own.
Contestant: Car.

Host: Besides an airplane, something man-made that flies.
Contestant: A jet.

Host: Name an article of clothing that children always lose.
Contestant: Pants.

From *Family Fortunes* (ITV):

Les Dennis: Name something a bridegroom might wear.
Contestant: Dress.

Les Dennis: Name a method of cooking fish.
Contestant: Cod.

Les Dennis: Name a form of transport you can walk around in.
Contestant: My foot.

Les Dennis: Name a game played in the dark.
Contestant: Charades.

Les Dennis: Name a famous Harry Enfield character.
Contestant: Sooty.

Les Dennis: Name a famous robber.
Contestant: Cops.

Les Dennis: Name a famous bridge.
Contestant: The Bridge over Troubled Waters.

Les Dennis: Name a holiday where men buy last-minute gifts for their wife.
Contestant: Bank holiday.

• •

From *Playing for Time* (BBC):

Eamonn Holmes: What letter is used twice in the word 'fillet'?
Contestant: Fish.

• •

From *Press Your Luck* (CBS):

Peter Tomarken: Franklin D. Roosevelt is found on the head side of what American coin?
Contestant: A fifty-dollar bill.

• •

From *Steve Wright in the Afternoon* (BBC Radio 2):

Steve Wright: Which month of the year is named after the Roman god of war?
Contestant: Thursday.

• •

From *The Weakest Link* (BBC):

Anne Robinson: Name a selection of small, highly coloured sweets known as Dolly …?
Contestant: Parton.

Anne Robinson: The title 'Countess' is given to the wife of which rank of the British nobility?
Contestant: Queen.

Anne Robinson: A wild guess is 'a shot in the …' what?
Contestant: 'Arm'.

Anne Robinson: Which 'M' describes exhibiting clothes or making Airfix aircraft?

Contestant: Hangar.

Anne Robinson: Which three-letter word is known as the definite article?

Contestant: 'It'?

From *The Weakest Link* (NBC):

Anne Robinson: How many red stripes are there on the American flag?

Contestant: Fifty.

Anne Robinson: What does the 'U' stand for in the name of the dissolved country USSR?

Contestant: Russia.

WITHERING
LOOKS

The following examples require you to picture the environment in which the quiz show takes place. Because sometimes it's not the hotness of the lights, nor the nerves induced by wanting all those glittering prizes, that causes contestants' brains to go on strike. It's not even the difficulty of the questions that inspires the greatest fear. It's the hosts themselves: the raised eyebrow and palpable ennui of Jeremy Paxman; the fiery glare and pointed smirk of Anne Robinson in her leather trenchcoat. And while there are apparently many people who find Paxo's steely manner vaguely sexy, one imagines there are times when it might be harder to swoon. Especially if you happen to forget the chemical formula for Hydrogen Sulphide. (It's H_2S. *Obviously*.)

Of course, on friendlier shows such as *Sale of the Century*, the hosts are more amenable. They flash their perfect white teeth, pretend to make friends with the contestants and gently nudge them towards the right answers if things get a bit hairy. You'd have to say something monumentally stupid, if not freakishly dense, to procure a withering look on a show like that. But what do you know? Those freakish intelligence-allergics really *do* exist.

● ●

From *Beg, Borrow or Steal* (BBC):

Jamie Theakston: Do you know where Cambridge University is?
Contestant: [laughing] No, geography is not my strong point.
Jamie Theakston: There's a clue in its title.
Contestant: Er … Leicester?

● ●

From *Bingo America* (GSN):

Richard Karn: Name a famous fictional bear.
Contestant: Polar?
Richard Karn: I'm sorry?
Contestant: Polar bear?
Richard Karn: Okaaaaay. Let's move on.

● ●

From *Sale of the Century* (NBC):

Host: What insect is commonly found hovering above lakes?
Contestant: Crocodiles?
Host: What?!
Contestant: [interrupting] Pass!

Host: This place is both a famous cathedral and a university.
Contestant: Pass.
Host: No, the answer was Notre-Dame.
Contestant: How am I supposed to know that? I'm from Indiana.

From *The Weakest Link* (BBC):

Anne Robinson: In prisoner of war camps during World War Two, what 'T' was the kind of underground passage that was frequently dug as a means of escape?

Contestant: Herbal tea?

Anne Robinson: Nearly … It was 'tunnel'.

Anne Robinson: [after the round had finished] Did you have a bit of difficulty with the question?

Contestant: Yeah, but you asked me a difficult question. Everyone else got really easy questions and the question you asked me was, like, a million years old.

Anne Robinson: No, no. Not quite a million years old. World War Two. Have you heard of that?

Contestant: It was after World War One.

Anne Robinson: Are you sure?

Contestant: Is this a trick question?

Anne Robinson: Which fictional film character in *Star Wars* called Jar Jar was voted the most irritating film character of all time?

Contestant: Zsa Zsa Gabor.

Anne Robinson: No, it wasn't Zsa Zsa Gabor. Because it was of course Jar Jar Binks.

Anne Robinson: In the Lord's Prayer, what word beginning with 'H' meaning 'blessed' comes before 'be thy name'?

Contestant: [quietly] Howard.

Anne Robinson: [incredulously] Pardon?

Contestant: [louder] Howard!

From *The Weakest Link* (NBC):

Anne Robinson: What is the largest country in the Americas?

Contestant: Asia?

Anne Robinson: Um, Asia is a continent.

Contestant: Well, I don't live there!

From *Wheel of Fortune* (ITV):

Puzzle: Weak Wilbur is so weak, he's the only man in the world who ever got injured by playing [blank]?

Contestant: Sex?

Host: You don't *play* at that, you *work* at it.

From *University Challenge* (BBC):

Jeremy Paxman: What is another name for 'cherry pickers' and 'cheesemongers'?

Contestant: Homosexuals.

Jeremy Paxman: No. They're regiments in the British Army, who will be very upset with you.

PASS THE ATLAS, DEAR

One of the commonest general knowledge failures on quiz shows seems to be a rank inability to identify and separate cities, countries and continents – not to mention knowing where any of these funny foreign places actually are on a map.

The trouble is, our idea of what constitutes 'foreign' or 'far away' seems foreigner and further away than ever before. One need only witness *Big Brother* contestants puzzling over an unlabelled atlas – merrily prodding Africa and wondering if it's Spain – to have these suspicions confirmed. Which is strange, because we are told that the wonder of the internet and the convenience of cheap flights have enveloped the world like a warm, friendly hug and made us all friends. Sadly, after reading the following answers, you may find yourself feeling rather less cosy. Indeed, you could be forgiven for thinking that no one knows where *anything* is anymore.

• •

From *Beat the Nation* (Channel 4):

Tim Brooke-Taylor: Brazil is a major country in which continent?
Contestant: Europe.

* *

From *Bingo America* (GSN):

Richard Karn: What city bills itself as the entertainment capital of the world?
Contestant: Universal Studios.

* *

From *Blockbusters* (ITV):

Bob Holness: What 'U' are the Eastern Europeans who originated the tradition of painting on Easter eggs?
Contestant: Yugoslavians.

* *

From *Dog Eat Dog* (BBC):

Ulrika Jonsson: Budapest is the capital of which European country?
Contestant: This might be a stupid question, but I thought Europe was a country?

* *

From *Family Feud* (CBS):

Host: Name a Scandinavian country.
Contestant: Australia.

> **Host:** Name a country in Africa.
> **Contestant:** South America.

Host: Name a sophisticated city.
Contestant: Japan.
Contestant 2: France.

Host: Name a Southern city.
Contestant: Georgia.

Host: Name a state beginning with the letter 'M'.
Contestant: Mexico.

Host: Name a vacation city where you would need a lot of money.
Contestant: Hawaii.

Host: Name a city with one of the world's greatest art collections.
Contestant: Europe.

Host: Name an ancient city.
Contestant: Greece.

Host: Name a country Americans admire.
Contestant: Europe.

Host: Name a country known for its beautiful beaches.
Contestant: Hawaii.

Host: Name a country starting with 'B'.
Contestant: Bostonia.

Host: Name a famous resort area outside of the continental United States.
Contestant: Tahoe.

Host: Name a country that has a lot of snow.
Contestant: Alaska.

Host: The state with the best beaches.
Contestant: Los Angeles.

Host: Name a city in Arizona.
Contestant: Tampa Bay.

Host: Besides America, a country starting with the letter 'A'.
Contestant: Asia/Amsterdam.

> **Host:** Name a fictional island.
> **Contestant:** Rhode Island.

Host: Name a country you'd like to visit if you spent a summer in Europe.
Contestant: Paris.

Host: A country you might go to on holiday and put on weight.
Contestant: Paris.

From *Family Fortunes* (ITV):

Les Dennis: Name a Parisian landmark.
Contestant: Hawaii.

Les Dennis: Name a city in the state of Georgia.
Contestant: Alabama.

From *Live & Kicking* (BBC):

Host: What is the highest mountain in Britain?
Contestant: Mount Everest.

From *Nation Vacation* (Nation217):

Host: Which of these is a city in Germany: Hanoi, Hannover or Hangover?
Contestant: Hanoi.

From *National Lottery Jet Set* (BBC):

Eamonn Holmes: What is the world's largest continent?
Contestant: The Pacific.

Eamonn Holmes: Which is the largest country in South America?
Contestant: Nairobi.

From *Press Your Luck* (CBS):

Peter Tomarken: 'If I can make it there, I can make it anywhere.' What city does that describe?
Contestant: Phoenix.

Peter Tomarken: Bourbon whiskey is named after Bourbon County, located in what state?
Contestant: England.

From *Steve Wright in the Afternoon* (BBC Radio 2):

Steve Wright: On which continent would you find the River Danube?
Contestant: India.

Steve Wright: What is the capital of Switzerland? Be careful with this one.
Contestant: Munich.

From *Steve Yabsley on the Loose* (BBC Radio Bristol):

Steve Yabsley: What's the highest mountain in the UK?
Contestant: Mount Etna.

From *This Morning with Richard and Judy* (ITV):

John Leslie: What is the capital of France?
Contestant: Belgium.

Judy Finnigan: Where's the Acropolis?
Contestant: Pass.

From *The Weakest Link* (BBC):

Anne Robinson: In Asian geography, Vietnam has borders with Laos, Cambodia and which other country?
Contestant: America.

Anne Robinson: In which city do we find the Kremlin building?
Contestant: Russia.

Anne Robinson: Pakistan was part of which other state until it achieved independence in 1947?
Contestant: Bulgaria.

Anne Robinson: In which city is the Scottish parliament situated?

Contestant: London.

Anne Robinson: In which continent is the River Danube?

Contestant: France.

> **Anne Robinson:** What is the capital of Iraq?
>
> **Contestant:** Iran.

Anne Robinson: In which country is the River Po?

Contestant: Poland.

Anne Robinson: Sri Lanka is situated to the south-east of which Asian country?

Contestant: South Africa.

Anne Robinson: The Benelux consists of Belgium, Luxembourg and which other country?

Contestant: Switzerland.

Anne Robinson: Which city was chosen to host the first Chinese Grand Prix in 2007?

Contestant: Tokyo.

Anne Robinson: Which country in South America is named after the explorer Simon Bolivar?

Contestant: Brazil.

Anne Robinson: Which country lies directly east of South Korea?

Contestant: North Korea.

Anne Robinson: Which German city is also the name of a type of perfume?

Contestant: Berlin.

Anne Robinson: Which is the largest and most heavily populated island in the Mediterranean sea?

Contestant: Spain.

> **Anne Robinson:** Which Italian city is overlooked by Vesuvius?
>
> **Contestant:** Bombay.

Anne Robinson: Which oriental country shares its name with a type of porcelain?

Contestant: Portugal.

Anne Robinson: Which port in Belgium serves as a port for Bruges?

Contestant: Zagreb.

Anne Robinson: Which 'S' is the only country to have a land border with Portugal?

Contestant: Pass.

Anne Robinson: Which South American country has borders with ten others?

Contestant: China.

Anne Robinson: What is the capital of Saudi Arabia?

Contestant: Tel Aviv.

> **Anne Robinson:** In which European city is the River Clyde?
> **Contestant:** Mexico?

Anne Robinson: What is the capital of Italy?
Contestant: Pass.

Anne Robinson: What was the last state to join the USA?
Contestant: Canada.

From *The Weakest Link* (NBC):

Anne Robinson: Which US state is home to the Boston Symphony Orchestra?
Contestant: Boston.

Anne Robinson: This city, whose name means 'Eastern Capital', is the capital of Japan.
Contestant: Hong Kong.

Anne Robinson: What is the capital of New Jersey?
Contestant: Delaware.

Anne Robinson: The Governor's Mansion in the state of Georgia is located in which city?
Contestant: Alabama.

> **Anne Robinson:** What is the most northerly city in the British Isles?
> **Contestant:** Italy.

• •

From *The Vault* (ITV):

Host: In which European city was the first opera house opened in 1637?
Contestant: Mexico?

• •

From BBC Radio Nottingham:

Host: In which country is Mount Everest?
Contestant: [after long pause] Um, it's not in Scotland, is it?

• •

From Q103 Cambridge:

Host: What is the county town of Kent?
Contestant: Don't know. Um, is it Kentish Town?

• •

From Star FM Cambridgeshire:

Host: In which country would you find Miami?
Contestant: Uh … Pass.

• •

CULTURAL INSENSITIVITY

While international banks proudly advertise the fact that they know how to do business abroad, most of us couldn't really say whether it's offensive to present gifts with your left hand in Africa (it is), or whether it's wrong to say the word 'fifteen' in Japan (it isn't, but 'fourteen' in Japanese sounds like 'death', so is best avoided). What if you wear blue shorts to the bank in Turkey? Does it make any difference if you do it on a Friday? And what happens if you also happen to be carrying a monkey or eating a cheese roll? Be careful, it's a complicated world out there.

In general, we can be forgiven for not knowing our way around these cultural differences – they're obscure, and that's why we have guidebooks. But the following quiz contestants might need a little more help than a travel guide can offer …

• •

From *The Dave Lee Travis Show* (Breeze FM):

Dave Lee Travis: In which European country are there people called Walloons?
Contestant: Wales.

From *Blockbusters* (ITV):

Bob Holness: What 'K' is a suicide mission for a pilot?
Contestant: *Kama Sutra.*

Bob Holness: What 'S' is the US's number-one import from
Manchuria?
Contestant: Spaghetti.

From *Cash Cab* (ITV):

John Moody: The Anne Frank Museum can be found in which
city?
Contestant: Berlin.

> **John Moody:** Name a famous Irishman.
> **Contestant:** Scruffy McMurphy.

• •

From *Dog Eat Dog* (BBC):

Ulrika Jonsson: Name the German national airline.
Contestant: The Luftwaffe.

• •

From *Family Feud* (CBS):

Host: Name a foreign country that you would want to visit.
Contestant: Afghanistan.

Host: Name an expression that means 'getting married'.
Contestant: Rendezvous.

Host: Name something that London is famous for.
Contestant: I'm thinking pasta?

Host: Name a city with a reputation as the sin capital of the
world.
Contestant: Sodom.

Host: Name a Jewish person that had a great impact on society.
Contestant: Mussolini.

Host: Name something that finishes the sentence: 'You're slower
than …'
Contestant: 'Moses'.

Host: Name something the English are famous for.
Contestant: Driving on the wrong side of the road.

Host: Name something this country imports too much of.
Contestant: Foreign goods.

From *Family Fortunes* (ITV):

Les Dennis: Name a character from the movie *Aladdin*.
Contestant: Jihad.

Les Dennis: Name a famous Irishman.
Contestant: Disraeli?

From *The Janice Forsyth Show* (BBC Radio Scotland):

Janice Forsyth: What is India's currency?
Contestant: Ramadan.

From *National Lottery Jet Set* (BBC):

Eamonn Holmes: What does the French phrase *Je t'aime* mean?
Contestant: 'Goodbye'.

From *Fifteen to One* (Channel 4):

William G. Stewart: New Zealand has two national anthems. One of them is 'God Save the Queen'. What's the other one?
Contestant: 'Australia Fair'.

William G. Stewart: Above the entrance to which place do the words 'Abandon all hope, all ye who enter here' appear?
Contestant: Is it a church?
William G. Stewart: No, it's hell.

From *See Hear on Saturday* (BBC):

Lara Crooks: What country does the spiritual leader the Dalai Lama come from?
Contestant: Scotland.

From *The Steve Penk Breakfast Show* (Virgin Radio):

Steve Penk: The name of the French-speaking Canadian state?
Contestant: America? Portugal? Canada? Mexico? Italy? Spain?

From *Steve Wright in the Afternoon* (BBC Radio 2):

Steve Wright: In England it's called petrol. What is it called in the United States?
Contestant: Diesel.

From *This Morning with Richard and Judy* (ITV):

Richard Madeley: [affecting woeful accent] Ze Moulin Rouge! In what seety can you find zis famoose night club, hee-haw hee-haw?
Contestant: Italy.

Colleen Nolan: To which member of the royal family is the Duke of Edinburgh married?
Contestant: Pass.

John Leslie: If you spoke Dutch, what country would you be from?
Contestant: Denmark.

From *The Weakest Link* (BBC):

Anne Robinson: *Achtung* is a word for 'warning' in which European language?
Contestant: Chinese.

Anne Robinson: In fashion, what is the French for 'ready to wear'?
Contestant: *Prêt à manger.*

Anne Robinson: In fashion, what does the term *prêt à porter* mean?
Contestant: 'Carrying clothes'.

Anne Robinson: What 'T' are people who live in a house paying rent to a landlord?
Contestant: Terrorists.

Anne Robinson: Mandarin and Cantonese are two languages that originated in which country?
Contestant: Spain.

> **Anne Robinson:** What religion was founded by the prophet Mohammed in AD 610?
> **Contestant:** Rastafarianism.

Anne Robinson: A Catalan is an inhabitant of a region in Spain known in English as what?
Contestant: Catatonia.

Anne Robinson: The cedar tree appears on the flag of which Middle Eastern country with a coastline on the Mediterranean?
Contestant: Canada.

Anne Robinson: The name of which Italian, born in 1469, is synonymous with immoral cunning?
Contestant: Mussolini.

Anne Robinson: What island nation was the book *Hiroshima* written about?
Contestant: Iwo Jima.

Anne Robinson: What 'K' is the currency of Sweden?
Contestant: Kennel.

Anne Robinson: In what language is the word *banzai* both a war cry and an address to the emperor?
Contestant: Chinese.

Anne Robinson: In what language, spoken in part of the United Kingdom, was the hymn 'Guide Me O Thou Great Redeemer' originally written?

Contestant: Islam.

Anne Robinson: Which country has the largest number of Portuguese speakers in the world?

Contestant: Spain.

Anne Robinson: Which Danish city is famous for its statue of a mermaid?

Contestant: Denmark.

Anne Robinson: Which European language do the words 'blitz', 'kindergarten' and 'angst' come from?

Contestant: Italian.

Anne Robinson: In politics, what is the current occupation of David Blunkett?

Contestant: Blind.

Anne Robinson: Which Indian leader, whose last name began with 'G', took the name Mahatma?

Contestant: Geronimo.

Anne Robinson: Who initiated the Chinese Cultural Revolution?

Contestant: Ming.

From *The Weakest Link* (NBC):

Anne Robinson: The name of what ceremony of the installation of a new monarch comes from the Latin for 'crown'?
Contestant: Head.

> **Anne Robinson:** What's the capital of France?
> **Contestant:** 'F'?

Anne Robinson: The name of which Caribbean island literally means 'rich port' in Spanish?
Contestant: Port Richmond.

Anne Robinson: What 'S' is one of the seven deadly sins in Christianity?
Contestant: Science.

Anne Robinson: In religion, the Jehovah's Witnesses distribute *Awake* and what other magazine?
Contestant: *MAD*.

Anne Robinson: Which Middle Eastern country's flag contains a line from the Qur'an over a sword on a green background?
Contestant: Israel.

From *Who Wants to Be a Millionaire?* (ITV):

Chris Tarrant: [asking the audience] *Jambon* is the French for which food?
11 per cent of audience: Jam.

From *University Challenge* (BBC):

Jeremy Paxman: What South American politician overthrew Allende in a coup?
Contestant: Ayatollah Khomeini?
Contestant 2: Chile?

> **Bamber Gascoigne:** What was Gandhi's first name?
> **Contestant:** Goosey?

From Beacon FM:

DJ Mark: For ten pounds, what is the nationality of the Pope?
Contestant: I think I know that one. Is it Jewish?

From Q103 Cambridge:

Host: What's the official language of China?
Contestant: Asian.

MISHAPS AND MISHEARS

On some quiz shows, control of the game is determined by how fast you are. So it is with *Family Fortunes* (or its American counterpart, *Family Feud*), where 100 random, ordinary people are asked to answer a simple survey. All the two families have to do is think like ordinary people and guess one of the most popular answers to each survey question. But speed is key, as the first family to answer wins the chance to fill in the rest of the blanks on the big board. And that leads to the big money.

So a member of each clan stands poised, one hand behind their back and the other hovering madly over the big red buzzer. It's a sort of battle – albeit a very silly one. But my, how thick and fast those pesky questions come along! One can't blame the contestants for being eager, even if their eventual answers verge on nonsense.

All this brings us neatly to the wonderful world of quiz show mishears, where words transform nonsensically into other, less sensible words – with what the TV industry likes to call 'hilarious results'.

From *Family Feud* (CBS):

Where 'claws' becomes 'Claus' …

Host: Name something with claws.
Contestant: Christmas?

Where 'phony' becomes 'pony' …

Host: Name something you might buy, that could turn out to be phony.
Contestant: A horse?

From *Family Fortunes* (ITV):

Where 'Arthur' becomes 'author' …

Les Dennis: Name a famous Arthur.
Contestant: Shakespeare?

Where 'money' becomes 'Mummy' (in rather an alarming way) …

Les Dennis: Name a slang word for money.
Contestant: Bitch?

> *Where 'bean' becomes 'bian' …*
>
> **Les Dennis:** Name a type of bean.
> **Contestant:** Les-bean?

Where 'hours' become 'R's …

Les Dennis: How many hours are there in three days?
Contestant: One?

Where 'black ball' becomes 'blackboard' …

Les Dennis: Name a game played with a black ball.
Contestant: Darts?

Where 'sea' becomes 'C' …

Les Dennis: Name something associated with the sea.
Contestant: Coffin?

From *Steve Wright in the Afternoon* (BBC Radio 2):

Where 'comet' becomes 'comic' …

Steve Wright: Which comet was last seen in 1986?
Contestant: Robin Williams?

ANIMAL
MAGIC

We have lived side by side with our furry/scaly/feathered friends since time began, so it seems reasonable to assume we'd know at least a little (if not everything, in the case of cats and dogs) about our four-legged or finned companions. Sadly, it seems we're more interested in their ability to sit on our laps, come to heel or fetch the paper. If a wild bear ever happened to wander into the average home, no doubt the inhabitants' first urge would be to teach it a cute trick. And then video it for YouTube.

Unbelievably, the fourth entry is not a typo. *Hamster eggs.*

●●

From *Blockbusters* (ITV):

Bob Holness: What 'T' can travel at speeds of up to 900 feet per second?
Contestant: Turtle.

Bob Holness: What 'W' has a brain the size of a cherry and can impact a tree at 1300mph?
Contestant: Water buffalo.

From *Cash Cab* (ITV):

John Moody: What is the only mammal capable of true flight?
Contestant: Pterodactyl.

From *Family Feud* (CBS):

Host: Name an animal whose eggs you'd never eat for breakfast.
Contestant: Hamster?

Host: Name a noisy bird.
Contestant: Chipmunk.

Host: Name an animal that begins with 'M'.
Contestant: Marsupial.

Host: Name an animal that begins with the letter 'E'.
Contestant: Ecuador.
Contestant 2: Iguana.
Contestant 3: Eggplant.

Host: Name an animal that starts with 'D', besides 'dog'.
Contestant: Dragon.

Host: Name something you associate with the sea.
Contestant: Crows.

Host: Name an animal with more than four legs.
Contestant: Dog?
Contestant 2: Horse.

Host: Name an animal with really good sight.
Contestant: Bat.

Host: Name an animal with three letters in its name.
Contestant: Frog.
Contestant 2: Alligator.

Host: Name something that you wanted to do as a kid, but your parents wouldn't let you.
Contestant: Have a snake?

Host: Name something that your dog does.
Contestant: Pees?
Contestant 2: Poops?

Host: Name something you hope your dog doesn't do right before he licks your head.
Contestant: Burps.

Host: The most lovable breed of dog.
Contestant: Kitten.

From *Family Fortunes* (ITV):

Les Dennis: Name something that's only useful when it's set.
Contestant: Dead animals. You know, when you want to stuff them?

Les Dennis: Name an animal you might see at a zoo.
Contestant: Dog.

Andy Collins: Name something Old Macdonald had on his farm.
Contestant: Giraffe.

> **Les Dennis:** Name something that makes you scream.
> **Contestant:** Squirrel?

Les Dennis: Name an animal that starts with the letter 'A'.
Contestant: Arachnophobia.

From *Press Your Luck* (CBS):

Peter Tomarken: What animal builds dams and lodges?
Contestant: Sheep.

From *Pyramid* (CBS):

Host: Name an animal that makes the noise 'gobble, gobble, gobble'.
Contestant: A chicken?

From *The Weakest Link* (BBC):

Anne Robinson: If you're superstitious, you salute which black and white bird when it is seen alone?
Contestant: Penguin.

Anne Robinson: In Roman mythology, which animal brought up Romulus and Remus?

Contestant: A lion.

Anne Robinson: In nature, cumulus and cirrus are types of what?

Contestant: Lion.

Anne Robinson: The name of which small, wingless, jumping insect precedes 'bite', 'collar', and 'market' to give three familiar terms?

Contestant: Bicycle.

Anne Robinson: In the animal kingdom, what 'C' is a large North American reindeer?

Contestant: A moose.

Anne Robinson: What does a bat use to facilitate flying in the dark?

Contestant: Its wings.

Anne Robinson: What is the correct name for the Australian wild dog?

Contestant: The dingbat.

Anne Robinson: Which bird gives its name to a straight-legged marching step?

Contestant: The cuckoo.

Anne Robinson: Which letter of the alphabet sounds exactly the same as the term for a female sheep?

Contestant: Baa.

Anne Robinson: Which large mammal is adapted to sandy conditions, having protective eyelashes, nostrils that can be closed, and broad, soft feet?

Contestant: Alligator.

• •

From *The Weakest Link* (NBC):

Anne Robinson: What 'T' is both an item of underwear and a rising column of warm air?
Contestant: Turtle.

• •

From *Who Wants to Be a Millionaire?* (ABC),
$100 question:

Regis Philbin: Which of the following is the largest:
a) A peanut; b) An elephant; c) The moon; d) A kettle?
Contestant: b) An elephant?

• •

WHOLE LOTTA HISTORY

In thirteen hundred and ninety-two,
Napoleon sailed the ocean blue.
He had ten cars and left from Dover;
His SatNav saved a lot of bother.

… or something like that, anyway.

Although not everybody enjoyed rote-learning history at school, and although all those kings and wars and draughty castles can quickly start blurring into one another, there are quite a lot of historical facts that fall under the heading 'The Bleeding Obvious'. Let's test that theory with a quick-fire round: Which English king had six wives? Henry VIII. Which country was once ruled by tsars? Russia. Who was the first man on the moon? Er … Louis Armstrong?

● ●

From *The Biggest Game in Town* (ITV):

Steve le Fevre: What was signed to bring World War I to an end in 1918?
Contestant: Magna Carta.

From *Dog Eat Dog* (BBC):

Ulrika Jonsson: Which US president was shot in 1981?
Contestant: J. F. Kennedy.

From *Family Feud* (CBS):

Host: Name a president who served two full terms.
Contestant: Abraham Lincoln.

Host: Name an important city during colonial times.
Contestant: Virginia.
Contestant 2: New England.

Host: Name someone who signed the Declaration of
  Independence.
Contestant: Thomas Edison.

From *Family Fortunes* (ITV):

Les Dennis: Name a weapon used in the ancient world.
Contestant: Hand grenade.

From *Fifteen to One* (Channel 4):

William G. Stewart: Now think carefully before you answer
  this. Where did Alexander the Great come from?
Contestant: Belgium.

From *The James O'Brien Show* (LBC):

James O'Brien: How many kings of England have been called Henry?

Contestant: Well, I know Henry VIII. So, um, three?

From *Sale of the Century* (ITV):

Host: How many Christmases took place during the Second World War?

Contestant: Fifty-eight?

Host: What is the name of the primitive language used by the Ancient Egyptians and painted on walls?

Contestant: Hydraulics.

Host: What was Hitler's first name?

Contestant: Heil.

From *Sale of the Century* (NBC):

Host: In 1955, a longtime rivalry ended when the AFL merged with what other trade union?

Contestant: The NFL.

From *Steve Wright in the Afternoon* (BBC Radio 2):

Steve Wright: In 1863, which American president gave the Gettysburg Address?

Contestant: I don't know, it was before I was born.

From *Studio 7* (The WB Network):

Pat Kiernan: Which former British colony was handed back to the Chinese in 1997?
Contestant: London.

From *The Tonight Show with Jay Leno* (NBC):

Jay Leno: Who was the first man on the moon?
Contestant: Louis Armstrong.

From *This Morning with Richard and Judy* (ITV):

Richard Madeley: Charles and Edward were children of whom?
Contestant: Diana.

Richard Madeley: When was the Battle of Hastings?
Contestant: 1866.

Judy Finnigan: Which country was ruled by tsars, France or Russia?
Contestant: France.

Richard Madeley: Which desert war did Britain take part in ten years ago today?
Contestant: The Falklands.

From *The Weakest Link* (BBC):

Anne Robinson: According to the Bible, what city was destroyed along with Gomorrah?
Contestant: Atlantis.

Anne Robinson: In ancient mythology, how many labours did Hercules have to tackle?

Contestant: One.

Anne Robinson: In Italy, in 1919, which former journalist set up the Fascist Party?

Contestant: Silvio Berlusconi.

Anne Robinson: In politics, what 'W' was a pact signed by the Soviet Union in 1955 as a response to West Germany joining NATO?

Contestant: The Williamsburg Treaty.

Anne Robinson: In the 1940s, which politician was responsible for the welfare state: William … who?

Contestant: The Conqueror.

Anne Robinson: In what year did the First World War end?
Contestant: 1948.

Anne Robinson: 'The Grapple in the Apple', recently held in New York, was a debate between the journalist Christopher Hitchens and the politician George ... who?
Contestant: George Washington.

Anne Robinson: What French word did Karl Marx use to describe those who oppressed the working class?
Contestant: Trotskyists.

Anne Robinson: What is the full name of Karl Marx's book: *Das* ... what?
Contestant: *Kampf.*

> **Anne Robinson:** Who wrote the political treatise *Das Kapital*?
> **Contestant:** John Major.

Anne Robinson: What is the round implement believed to have been invented around 4000 years ago and used in transport ever since?
Contestant: The steam engine.

Anne Robinson: What word for an Ancient Roman marketplace is also a site on the internet for open discussion?
Contestant: Chat room.

Anne Robinson: In which century was Hadrian's Wall built?
Contestant: The eighteenth century.

Anne Robinson: Name the man who was president of Italy until May 2006.

Contestant: Don Corleone.

Anne Robinson: Name the Empress of Russia who ruled between 1762 and 1796, famous for the number of her lovers.

Contestant: Boadicea.

Anne Robinson: Hadrian's Wall was built to keep out which tribe, the Picts or the Zulus?

Contestant: The Zulus.

Anne Robinson: Which Allied leader met with Roosevelt and Stalin at Yalta in 1945?

Contestant: Hitler.

Anne Robinson: Which British prime minister famously said, 'We have become a grandmother'?

Contestant: John Major.

From *The Weakest Link* (NBC):

Anne Robinson: The Nuremberg war crime trials were held in what country?

Contestant: Warsaw.

Anne Robinson: What Tennessee congressman fought at the Battle of the Alamo?

Contestant: Al Gore.

Anne Robinson: According to legend, who rode naked through the streets of Coventry to protest high taxes?

Contestant: Benjamin Franklin.

Anne Robinson: Who served as both vice-president and president without being elected to either office?

Contestant: Colin Powell.

Anne Robinson: In 1973, President Nixon issued a statement saying 'I am not a …' what?

Contestant: 'Canadian'.

* *

**From *Who Wants to Be a Millionaire?* (ABC),
$1000 question:**

Regis Philbin: As part of its maintenance, which of these tourist attractions requires the use of embalming fluid: a) Lenin's Tomb; b) Mount Rushmore; c) Stonehenge; d) Hoover Dam?

Contestant: c) Stonehenge, final answer.

Regis Philbin: Noooooo, I'm sorry. Embalming fluid is used at Lenin's Tomb.

Contestant: There, of all places!

* *

From BBC Radio Nottingham:

Host: Where did the D-Day landings take place?

Contestant: [after pause] Pearl Harbor?

* *

AND THE OSCAR GOES TO …

Perhaps the explanation behind the following quiz-question flops is that our contestants have immersed themselves *so* fully in celluloid drama that they've got real life and fantasy rather mixed up. Indeed, they're so engaged that they've forgotten film-making requires directors, smooth-talking producer types and, you know, actors. One assumes this is why they think James Bond is played by James Bond, that Carrie Bradshaw is a real person, and that Austin Powers famously made the, er, Austin Powers role his own. It's a theory. I didn't say it was good one.

• •

From *Cash Cab* (ITV):

John Moody: Who played Austin Powers in *Austin Powers: The Spy Who Shagged Me*?
Contestant: Austin Powers.

John Moody: In *Star Wars*, what peacekeeping force includes the ranks Padawan and Knight?
Contestant: Space Invaders.

. . . .

From *Bingo America* (GSN):

Richard Karn: Name an insect that grows to horrific
proportions in sci-fi movies.
Contestant: Lobster.

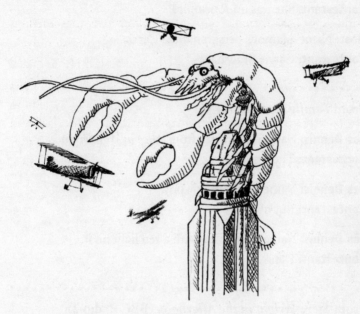

. . . .

From *Family Feud* (CBS):

Host: Name an actor who played a gangster.
Contestant: Al Capone.

. . . .

Host: Name the talent show with the moodiest judges, past or
present.
Contestant: *Animals Do the Funniest Things.*

> **Host:** Name a character from a horror movie that reminds you of someone you dated.
> **Contestant:** Loch Ness Monster.

Host: The one thing people know about Rosie O'Donnell.
Contestant: She was on *Roseanne*?

Host: Name a famous person named Carrie.
Contestant: Carrie Bradshaw.

From *Family Fortunes* (ITV):

Les Dennis: Name a character from *Alice in Wonderland*.
Contestant: The Tin Man.

Les Dennis: Name a famous cowboy.
Contestant: Buck Rogers.

Les Dennis: Name something with a red light on it.
Contestant: Dalek.

From *Steve Wright in the Afternoon* (BBC Radio 2):

Steve Wright: Who played agent 007 in the 1989 film *Licence To Kill*?
Contestant: Err … James Bond?

Steve Wright: Johnny Weissmuller died on this day. Which jungle-swinging character clad only in a loincloth did he play?
Contestant: Jesus.

From *This Morning with Richard and Judy* (ITV):

Fern Britton: Which actress starred in *Sleepless in Seattle* and *When Harry Met Sally*?
Contestant: Tom Hanks.

From *The Weakest Link* (BBC):

Anne Robinson: Gotham is not only a place in the Batman series, but also a city in which European country?
Contestant: Italy.

Anne Robinson: In the TV series of the same name, who played the pathologist Quincy?
Contestant: Quincy.

Anne Robinson: What is the name of the long-running TV comedy show about pensioners: *Last of the* ... what?

Contestant: *Mohicans.*

Anne Robinson: The director of the 1956 film *The Ten Commandments* was Cecil B. ... who?

Contestant: Parkinson.

Anne Robinson: In comedy, Ernie Wise was frequently teased by Eric Morecambe for having short, fat, hairy what?

Contestant: Hair.

Anne Robinson: Which iconic cartoon family made their film debut in 2007, twenty years after their show was first broadcast on American television?

Contestant: *The Osbournes.*

Anne Robinson: What is the name of the 1994 Oscar-winning film which starred Ben Kingsley as Itzhak Stern?

Contestant: *Gandhi.*

Anne Robinson: The role of the plump teenager Tracy Turnblad, played by Nikki Blonsky in the 2007 film *Hairspray*, was played in the 1988 original by Ricki ... who?

Contestant: Tomlinson.

Anne Robinson: What was the sequel to the movie *I Know What You Did Last Summer*?

Contestant: *I Know What You Did Last Winter.*

Anne Robinson: What is the title of the full-length feature film directed by *Wallace and Gromit* creator Nick Park?

Contestant: *Groundhog Day.*

Anne Robinson: What part did the Tin Man ask Dorothy to get him?

Contestant: A brain.

Anne Robinson: What was the title of the movie directed by James Cameron that starred Leonardo DiCaprio?

Contestant: *On the Beach.*

Anne Robinson: Which movie ended with the famous words, 'It was beauty that killed the beast'?

Contestant: Pass.

Anne Robinson: What was the title of the play *La Cage aux Folles* when it was remade into a movie starring Robin Williams?

Contestant: *Mrs Doubtfire.*

Anne Robinson: Which actress was married to Humphrey Bogart, and is also the cousin of former Israeli prime minister Shimon Peres?

Contestant: Gene Kelly.

Anne Robinson: Which Christina is an actress who made her debut in 1990 with the film *Mermaids*?

Contestant: Christina Aguilera.

Anne Robinson: In which film did Dudley Moore star as the title character?

Contestant: *10.*

Anne Robinson: Kate Hudson is the daughter of which famous American movie actress?

Contestant: Rock.

Anne Robinson: In which film did Harry Lime say, 'In Switzerland they had brotherly love and they had 500 years of democracy and peace. And what did they produce? The cuckoo clock'?

Contestant: *One Flew Over the Cuckoo Clock?*

From *The Weakest Link* (NBC):

Anne Robinson: In literature, Arthur C. Clarke's *2010: Odyssey Two* was primarily set in what century?

Contestant: Third.

Anne Robinson: On TV's *Cheers*, which actress played bar manager Rebecca Howe?

Contestant: Ted Danson.

Anne Robinson: On TV's *The Simpsons*, Homer's neighbour Ned had what last name?

Contestant: Barfbag?

Anne Robinson: What former child actor played the sympathetic Cornelius in the original *Planet of the Apes*?

Contestant: Gary Coleman.

Anne Robinson: Which William discovered that blood circulates around the body?

Contestant: Shatner.

> **Anne Robinson:** From which country is Sean Connery?
> **Contestant:** Germany.

Anne Robinson: In the USA, an unidentified dead body is sometimes known as a John … what?
Contestant: Wayne.

Anne Robinson: Who is the only Marx brother that remained silent throughout all their films?
Contestant: Karl.

From *University Challenge* (BBC):

Jeremy Paxman: Dubbed 'The Sphinx' in the 1920s on account of her taciturn manner off-screen, which Hollywood actress retired from public life in 1941?
Contestant: Julie Andrews.

From BBC Radio Nottingham:

Host: Name some famous brothers.
Contestant: Bonnie and Clyde.

From RTE Radio 2 FM:

Host: Name the film starring Bob Hoskins that is also the name of a famous painting by Leonardo Da Vinci.
Contestant: *Who Framed Roger Rabbit?*

THE END OF THE PIER

Where do mother-in-law jokes go to die? Quiz shows, apparently, for this is where things get ever so slightly un-PC – if not actively scatological. And though there might be something vaguely depressing about the spirit of Bernard Manning returning to haunt the annals of general ignorance, take heart in the knowledge that most of these examples are from way back in the 1970s and 1980s. And we were allowed to be sexist and gross then, weren't we?

From *Family Feud* (CBS):

Host: Name a bad habit that has serious consequences.
Contestant: Picking your nose.

> **Host:** Name a bad place to look for good husband material.
> **Contestant:** Funeral.

Host: Name a road sign that describes your love life.
Contestant: Slippery When Wet.

Host: Name a slang term for a man.
Contestant: The greater sex.

Host: Name something a man might buy his girlfriend a pair of.
Contestant: Boobs.

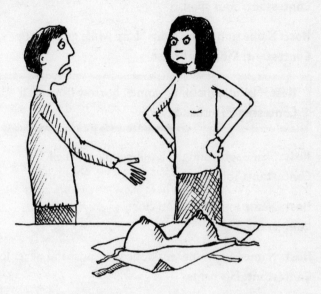

Host: Name something a man might do to look good that he
doesn't want people to know about.
Contestant: Stuff his pants.

Host: Name something a teenage boy can do for hours.
Contestant: Masturbate.

Host: Name something a wife tells her husband to put on.
Contestant: Make-up.

Host: Name something most women wouldn't be caught
leaving the house without.
Contestant: Tampon.

Host: Name something of yours that you hit when it's not working properly.
Contestant: Your spouse.

Host: Name something twins share while growing up.
Contestant: Mother's breast.

Host: Name something women borrow from each other.
Contestant: Husbands.

Host: Name something you ask people to smell.
Contestant: Your finger.

Host: Name something you close.
Contestant: Legs.

Host: Name something you hope your husband never loses.
Contestant: His pants.

Host: Name something you like that is bad for you.
Contestant: Sex.

Host: Name something you shouldn't try even once.
Contestant: Sex on a train.

Host: Name something you wouldn't use if it was dirty.
Contestant: Toilet paper.

Host: Name something you'd hate to be doing on an airplane when it hits turbulence.
Contestant: Having sex.

Host: Name something you'd hate to find out about the guy you almost married.

Contestant: He's a she.

Host: Name something your partner can't do without.

Contestant: Sex.

Host: Name something of yours you hope doesn't start making noises.

Contestant: Your dog.

Contestant 2: Your children.

Host: Name something people peek through.

Contestant: Down a lady's blouse.

> **Host:** Name something that can damage a home.
> **Contestant:** A woman.

Host: Name something someone does that annoys everyone in the room.

Contestant: Fart.

Host: Name something that gets wet when you use it.

Contestant: Toilet paper.

Host: Name something that has to warm up before you use it.

Contestant: Wife.

Host: Name something that works better after it's been broken in.

Contestant: Husband.

Host: Name something that you have to do to get your husband's attention during the Super Bowl.
Contestant: Take off your clothes.

Host: Name something you rent for one day.
Contestant: A stripper.

Host: Name something you should do in moderation or you'll be sorry later.
Contestant: Sex.

Host: Name something you shouldn't do in someone else's car.
Contestant: Fart.
Contestant 2: Get arrested.
Contestant 3: Throw up.

Host: Name something you wash once a week.
Contestant: Self.

Host: Where or when might you be scolded for falling asleep.
Contestant: Traffic school/During sex.

Host: The bad habit you'd most like to get rid of.
Contestant: Picking my nose.

Host: The birthday that men dread the most.
Contestant: Their wife's.

Host: The one thing that the people living near you have, that you want.
Contestant: A beautiful wife.

> **Host:** Name a famous pig.
> **Contestant:** My mother-in-law.

Host: The first thing you take off after work.
Contestant: Underwear.

Host: Name an excuse you might use when stopped for speeding.
Contestant: 'I was drinking.'

Host: Name an occasion when it would be noticed that you are late.
Contestant: Funeral.

Host: Name an occupation where you can make a lot of money without a lot of brains.
Contestant: A drug dealer.

Host: Name something that guests get hit with on *Jerry Springer*.
Contestant: Keys.

Host: Name something associated with pigs.
Contestant: The police.

From *Family Fortunes* (ITV):

Les Dennis: Name something you would do if you ran out of clean underpants.
Contestant: Sprinkle on some talcum powder.

Les Dennis: Name something that goes up.
Contestant: An erection.

Les Dennis: Name something you have with coffee.
Contestant: The *Sunday Sport*.

> **Les Dennis:** Name something you trim.
> **Contestant:** Feet.

Les Dennis: Name something you might do in a lift.
Contestant: Wee.

Les Dennis: Name something you open other than a door.
Contestant: Bowels.

Les Dennis: Name something people take from hotels as a souvenir.
Contestant: Lamps.

From *Press Your Luck* (CBS):

Peter Tomarken: According to the old saying, 'I scream, you scream, we all scream for …' what?
Contestant: 'Jim Beam'.

From *The Weakest Link* (BBC):

Anne Robinson: What 'A' is a small dead-end tube in the digestive system with no known function?
Contestant: Arse.

From *Richard & Judy* (ITV):

Richard Madeley: You step in it, and it takes you up and down to different floors. What is it?
Contestant: Dog poo?

NAUGHTY BY NATURE

Surveys have claimed that the average man thinks about sex nearly 5000 times a year, or thirteen times a day. Perhaps these statistics explain why there is such a lot of frisk and naughtiness on your average quiz show. After all, most of the contestants in this book appear to have answered with the first thing that came into their heads …

But that doesn't really explain the sauce that seems to emanate from female quiz contestants (who only think about 'it' five times a day, apparently). Nor the regularity with which contestants' answers slip below the belt and enter a post-watershed area. Indeed, it's almost as if canny quiz-show producers have cottoned on to the hilarity that ensues when a contestant's answer borders on the bawdy. Could they – *would they* – set up questions that are specifically designed to elicit risqué answers …?

• •

From *Bingo America* (GSN):

Richard Karn: At a cannibal Halloween party, instead of bobbing for apples, they bob for what?
Contestant: Boobs?

From *Dog Eat Dog* (BBC):

Ulrika Jonsson: In the well-known tongue twister, 'She sells ...' what?
Contestant: 'Knickers'.

From *Family Feud* (CBS):

Host: Name a famous sex symbol.
Contestant: Wilma.

Host: Name someone a married man might claim his mistress is, if he was caught in public with her.
Contestant: The cheerleader next door.

Host: Name something you'd open with your teeth.
Contestant: Zipper?

> **Host:** Name an occupation where someone wears a robe at work.
> **Contestant:** Prostitute.

Host: Name a magazine that many men get subscriptions to as gifts.
Contestant: *Playgirl.*

Host: Name a place where you might see another person take off all their clothes.
Contestant: The mall.

Host: Name a question that a gentleman would never ask a lady on a first date.

Contestant: 'What colour underwear do you wear?'

Host: Name a question you can't stand people to ask.

Contestant: 'Are those real?'

Host: Name a subject people discuss on their first date.

Contestant: Sex.

Host: Name a weather term that can also describe your wife.

Contestant: Wet.

Host: Name a party game that would be more fun to play in the nude.

Contestant: Monopoly.

Contestant 2: Chess.

Host: Name a word that rhymes with 'cookie'.
Contestant: 'Nookie'.

> **Host:** Name something books tell you that you can do in thirty days or less.
> **Contestant:** Make a baby.

Host: Name an excuse that a girl might give to not invite you into her home after a date.
Contestant: Her husband is home.

Host: Name an occasion for which you stayed up all night.
Contestant: Lost virginity.

Host: Name something a dentist says.
Contestant: 'Just a small prick.'

Host: Name something a man wears to bed.
Contestant: Condom.

Host: Name something a woman buys to spice up the romance at home.
Contestant: Whipped cream.

Host: Name something an Indian chief might use.
Contestant: Squaw.

Host: Name something bad you wouldn't think about.
Contestant: Sex.

Host: Name something Charlie Brown might do.
Contestant: Snoopy.

Host: Name something newlyweds share.
Contestant: Underwear.

Host: Name something that might get blocked up.
Contestant: Your body.

Host: Name something you do once a week.
Contestant: Make love.

Host: Name a body part that gets bigger as people get older.
Contestant: Penis.

Host: Name a department in a supermarket.
Contestant: Lingerie.

Host: Name something on a chihuahua that's tiny.
Contestant: Its Peter. [As in 'Peter Pecker', slang for penis.]

Host: Name something deserted in winter.
Contestant: My sister.

Host: Name something people associate with a sumo wrestler.
Contestant: Exposed buttocks?

Host: Name something people do clothed that others don't.
Contestant: Ride a motorcycle.

Host: Name something people do when they're alone.
Contestant: Make love.

Host: Name something that is prohibited on most beaches.
Contestant: Sex.

Host: How often do newlywed couples make love?
Contestant: Three times a day.

Host: Name a place where you wouldn't expect to meet a nun.
Contestant: Brothel.

From *Family Fortunes* (ITV):

Les Dennis: Name a game played in bed.
Contestant: Hide and seek?
Contestant 2: Tents.
Contestant 3: Trampoline?

Les Dennis: Name an article of clothing a woman might
borrow from a man.
Contestant: Underpants.

From *The Newlywed Game* (ABC):

Bob Eubanks: Where's the strangest place you've made whoopee?
Contestant: Up the ass?

BAD SPORTS

It's easy to feel sympathy for the contestants in this chapter, especially if you're the sort of person who'd rather have darts thrown at them than watch the World Darts on TV. But even those of us who assiduously avoid championships of any kind know that if you spell the famous racehorse Red Rum's name backwards you get 'murder'. I mean, that's not even a sports question. *The answer's right there in front of you.*

Suppose, however, that your brain doesn't have a sports department, and on top of that you suddenly find yourself on live TV talking to Judy – Judy Finnigan! Of *Richard and Judy*! No wonder, then, that when she says 'number' and 'wheels' and 'unicycle' in the same question, you're overwhelmed by an urge to blurt out 'Three!' It's OK, nobody's judging …

• •

From *Family Feud* (CBS):

Host: Name something people cheat on.
Contestant: Chicago Bears.

Host: The hardest position to play on a baseball team.
Contestant: Quarterback.

Host: Name a sport that involves throwing something.
Contestant: Tennis.

Host: Name something you associate with the Dallas Cowboys.
Contestant: Cowboy hats.

From *Family Fortunes* (ITV):

Les Dennis: Name a game that uses a black ball.
Contestant: Hockey.
Contestant 2: Darts.

> **Les Dennis:** Name an annual sporting event.
> **Contestant:** Running.

Les Dennis: Name an annual sporting event.
Contestant: The Olympics.

Les Dennis: Name a game you can play in the bath.
Contestant: Scuba diving.

From *National Lottery Jet Set* (BBC):

Eamonn Holmes: In 1994, what sporting event was cancelled due to a players' strike?
Contestant: China.

From *Press Your Luck* (CBS):

Peter Tomarken: Prior to 1984, what was the last year the United States participated in the Summer Olympics?
Contestant: 1936.

Peter Tomarken: What vehicle is used in the Tour de France race?
Contestant: SUVs.

From *The Weakest Link* (BBC):

Anne Robinson: He was known as the King of the Cowboys. He was Roy ... who?
Contestant: Keane.

Anne Robinson: In sport, the name of which famous racehorse was the word 'murder' spelt backwards?
Contestant: Shergar.

Anne Robinson: What implement is used to warn athletes that they are about to start the final lap?
Contestant: Starter gun.

Anne Robinson: Where was the recent Winter Olympics held?
Contestant: Taunton.

From *The Weakest Link* (NBC):

Anne Robinson: In what year of the 90s did badminton and
basketball become Olympic medal sports?
Contestant: 1984.

> **Anne Robinson:** What twenty-year-old Russian tennis star
> released a fitness video called *Basic Elements*?
> **Contestant:** Arnold Schwarzenegger.

Anne Robinson: Which figure skater was implicated in the 1994
attack on Olympic teammate Nancy Kerrigan?
Contestant: Monica Lewinsky.

From *This Morning with Richard
and Judy* (ITV):

Judy Finnigan: How many wheels
are there on a unicycle?
Contestant: Three.

CLUES AND CHEATS

There is a very rare breed of quiz show host characterized by kindness and generosity. They're so eager to give away the car, money or concert tickets that they'll do pretty much anything to get the contestant to say the right thing. They will hint, they will *more than hint*, if necessary.

But sadly there's little hope for the players in this chapter, as it seems no amount of help will get them closer to what's written on the answer card, even if our host literally spells out the answer, syllable by syllable, rather like an extremely patient game of Charades.

●●●

From *24-Hour Challenge* (BBC Radio York):

Jonathan Cowap: If someone is described as hirsute, what are they?

Contestant: Erm …

Jonathan Cowap: Here's a clue: most men are, and most women would like us to think they are not.

Contestant: Is it gay, Jonathan?

Jonathan Cowap: No.

From *Blockbusters* (ITV):

Bob Holness: What 'L' do you make in the dark, when you don't consider the consequences?
Contestant: Love?
Bob Holness: No, I'm sorry, I'm afraid the actual answer was 'leap'.

From *Chris Moyles' Breakfast Show* (BBC Radio 1):

Chris Moyles: Which 'S' is a kind of whale that can grow up to eighty tonnes?
Contestant: Umm …
Chris Moyles: It begins with 'S' and rhymes with 'perm'.
Contestant: Shark.

From *The Chris Searle Show* (BBC Radio Bristol):

Chris Searle: In which European country is Mount Etna?
Contestant: Japan.
Chris Searle: I did say which European country, so in case you didn't hear that, I can let you try again.
Contestant: Er … Mexico?

From *Dale's Supermarket Sweep* (ITV):

Dale Winton: Skegness is a seaside resort on the coast of which sea: a) Irish Sea; b) English Channel; c) North Sea?
Contestant: Oh, I know – and you can start writing out the cheque now. It's on the east coast, so it must be the Irish Sea.

• •

From *The Danny Kelly Show* (Radio WM):

Danny Kelly: Which French Mediterranean town hosts a famous film festival every year?

Contestant: Um, I think I need a clue.

Danny Kelly: OK. What do beans come in?

Contestant: Um, is it cartons?

• •

From *Daryl Denham's Drivetime* (Virgin Radio):

Daryl Denham: In which country would you spend shekels?

Contestant: Holland?

Daryl Denham: Try the next letter of the alphabet.

Contestant: Iceland? Ireland?

Daryl Denham: [helpfully] It's a bad line. Did you say Israel?

Contestant: No.

• •

From *Family Fortunes* (ITV):

Les Dennis: Name a Native American tribe.

Contestant: Um … [tries to peer at the card in the host's hand]

Les Dennis: Um, what about the Sigh-ooks?

Contestant: No, I think what you're trying to read there is 'Sioux'.

Les Dennis: Name a red liquid.

Contestant: Mercury?

Les Dennis: Is mercury red? Let's see if it's there. No, bad luck. I didn't think mercury was red.

Contestant: Yes, I wasn't sure if it was red or green.

From *Family Feud* (CBS):

Host: Name a part of the mouth.
Contestant: Tail?
Host: Tail?!
Contestant: Did you say mouth or mouse?
Host: Mouth! Oh, OK, give it another try, then.
Contestant: Nose?

From *The Late Show* (BBC Midlands Radio):

Alex Trelinski: What is the capital of Italy?
Contestant: France.
Alex Trelinski: France is another country. Try again.
Contestant: Oh, um, Benidorm.
Alex Trelinski: Wrong, sorry, let's try another question. In which country is the Parthenon?
Contestant: Sorry, I don't know.
Alex Trelinski: Just guess a country, then.
Contestant: Paris.

From *The Mick Girdler Show* (BBC Radio Solent):

Mick Girdler: I'm looking for an island in the Atlantic whose name includes the letter 'E'.
Contestant: Ghana.
Mick Girdler: No, listen. It's an island in the Atlantic Ocean.
Contestant: New Zealand.

• •

From *National Lottery Jet Set* (BBC):

Eamonn Holmes: What type of creature is a praying mantis?
Contestant: A fish.
Eamonn Holmes: Hmm. Are you sure you want to say fish?
Contestant: [confidently] Yes, definitely a fish.

• •

From *The Neil Pringle Show* (BBC Southern Counties Radio):

Neil Pringle: How many strings does a guitar have?
Contestant: Err … Four.
Neil Pringle: It's the number of wives that Henry VIII had …
Contestant: Oh! Five.

• •

From *The Phil Wood Show* (BBC Greater Manchester Radio):

Phil Wood: What 'K' could be described as the Islamic Bible?
Contestant: Err …
Phil Wood: It's got two syllables … Kor- …?
Contestant: Blimey?
Phil Wood: Ha ha ha ha, no. The past participle of 'run' …
Contestant: [silence]
Phil Wood: OK, try it another way. Today I run, yesterday I …?
Contestant: Walked?

From *Perseverance* (ITV):

Andrew Castle: What is the only even prime number? Two, four, six, or eight?
Contestant: Four.
Andrew Castle: Er, try again?
Contestant: Six.

From *Quizmania* (ITV):

Greg Scott: We're looking for a word that goes in front of 'clock'.
Contestant: Grandfather?
Greg Scott: Grandfather clock is already up there, try something else.
Contestant: Panda?

Greg Scott: We're looking for an occupation beginning with 'T'.
Contestant: Doctor.
Greg Scott: No, it's 'T'. 'T' for Tommy. 'T' for Tango.
Contestant: Oh, right … [pause] … Doctor.

From *Radio Hallam Breakfast Show* (Sheffield):

Host: Of which European country is Lisbon the capital?
Contestant: Australia.
Host: Sorry, that's the wrong answer; we'll go to the next caller.
Contestant 2: I was going to say Australia as well. Is it Gibraltar?
Host: No.

From *Simply the Best* (ITV):

Phil Tufnell: How many Olympic Games have there been?
Contestant: Six.
Phil Tufnell: Higher!
Contestant: Five.

From *Steve Wright in the Afternoon* (BBC Radio 2):

Steve Wright: How many days are there in five weeks?
Contestant: Don't know.
Steve Wright: Give it a guess.
Contestant: Sixty.

Steve Wright: What is the capital of Australia?
Contestant: Um …
Steve Wright: It's not Sydney.
Contestant: [long pause] Um … Sydney?

From *This Morning with Richard and Judy* (ITV):

John Leslie: On which street did Sherlock Holmes live?
Contestant: [silence]
John Leslie: He makes bread?
Contestant: Err …
John Leslie: He makes cakes …
Contestant: Kipling Street?
John Leslie: Um, no.

John Leslie: In 2002, the Queen celebrated her Golden Jubilee. So in which year did she come to the throne?

Contestant: 1958.

John Leslie: No, it was 1952. Fair enough – I mean, I wouldn't have got that.

Contestant: No, it was far too hard.

John Leslie: The Berlin Wall was demolished in which country?

Contestant: Um …

John Leslie: East and West came together?

Contestant: Err …

John Leslie: It begins with a 'G'?

Contestant: Err … [silence]

John Leslie: No, I'm sorry, I can't give you that one.

Richard Madeley: Who wrote *Othello*?

Contestant: No idea.

Richard Madeley: He also wrote *Hamlet*.

Contestant: Pass.

Richard Madeley: In which US state can you find Los Angeles, San Francisco and lots of big bears?

Contestant: Florida.

Richard Madeley: No, it's on the other side.

Judy Finnigan: [sings] 'I wish they all could be *da-da-da-da* girls.'

Contestant: New York?

Richard Madeley: Who sang 'New York, New York' and 'Chicago'?

Contestant: Err …

Richard Madeley: His nickname was 'Old Blue Eyes'.

Contestant: I don't know.

Richard Madeley: Who was Bill Clinton's vice-president?

Contestant: I don't know.

Richard Madeley: Come on, he also stood for president himself. You know, Al …

Contestant: Al Jolson.

Richard Madeley: Whom did Britain go to war with over the Falklands?

Contestant: Err …

Richard Madeley: It's a South American country.

Contestant: Iran.

Judy Finnigan: The American TV show *The Sopranos* is about opera. True or false?

Contestant: True?

Judy Finnigan: No, actually, it's about the Mafia. But it *is* an American TV show, so I'll give you that.

John Leslie: In what year did the Second World War start?

Contestant: 1918.

John Leslie: No, the Second World War. Have another try.

Contestant: Er … 1937?

John Leslie: What kind of creature is a halibut?

Contestant: A bird.

John Leslie: No, wrong. Try again.

Contestant: A ferret?

John Leslie: What's the Prince of Wales's Christian name?

Contestant: Um … Don't know.

John Leslie: Here's a clue: he was married to Diana.

Contestant: Err …

John Leslie: It begins with a 'C'?

Contestant: No, no idea.

From *Who Wants to Be a Millionaire?* (MBC1), 200 Saudi riyals question:

George Kurdahi: What is the total number of world wars up until today: a) One world war; b) Two world wars; c) Three world wars; d) Four world wars?

Contestant: I'm going to have to use my 50:50 lifeline.

[They take away two wrong answers, leaving two remaining possible answers: b) Two world wars; d) Four world wars.]

Contestant: I don't want to lose another lifeline, so I think I'll say d), four world wars.

George Kurdahi: Well, it's a difficult question.

[Laughter from studio audience.]

Contestant: Hmm. I know there was a World War One and a World War Two. So now I am trying to remember if there were any more world wars. [Thinks, titters from studio audience.] Yes, sorry, there have only been two, haven't there? Sorry, everyone.

From BBC Radio Norfolk:

Stewart White: Who had a worldwide hit with 'It's a Wonderful World'?

Contestant: I don't know.

Stewart White: I'll give you a couple of clues. What do you call the part between your hand and your elbow?

Contestant: Arm?

Stewart White: Correct. And if you're not weak, you're …?

Contestant: Strong?

Stewart White: Correct. And what was Lord Mountbatten's first name?

Contestant: Louis.

Stewart White: Well, there we are, then. So who had a worldwide hit with the song 'It's a Wonderful World'?

Contestant: Frank Sinatra?

From Lincs FM:

Host: Which is the largest Spanish-speaking country in the world?

Contestant: Barcelona.

Host: I was really after the name of a country.

Contestant: I'm sorry, I don't know the names of any countries in Spain.

From BRMB 96.4 FM:

Host: What religion was Guy Fawkes?
Contestant: Jewish.
Host: That's close enough.

From Magic 52 Radio:

Host: In what year was President Kennedy assassinated?
Contestant: Erm …
Host: Well, let's put it this way: he didn't see 1964.
Contestant: 1965?

From TalkSPORT Radio:

Andy Townsend: How many wheels does a tricycle have?
Contestant: Two.
Andy Townsend: The Beatles were known as the 'Fab …'?
Contestant: 'Five'.

RANDOM REVELATIONS

Sometimes, contestants' wrong answers are rather strange and revealing, as if the contents of their brains are even weirder than you might at first have suspected. And when faced with answers as random as those that follow, one starts to wonder whether these people are really quite alright; whether they're of sound mind and body, or whether some sort of rudimentary psychological test might be in order before they're let loose on the buzzer. What, for example, can our first *Family Feud* contestant possibly have been up to in his spare time? Does he have a confession to make?

• •

From *Bingo America* (GSN):

Richard Karn: What's the longest you've ever been on the telephone?
Contestant: Alaska.

Richard Karn: After a seventy-six-year absence, what comet last appeared in 1986?
Contestant: Spider-Man.

> **Richard Karn:** Where is the Taj Mahal?
> **Contestant:** [deadpan] Opposite the dental hospital?

From *Cash Cab* (ITV):

John Moody: What's the ideal daily temperature?
Contestant: 98.6F?

From *Dog Eat Dog* (BBC One):

Ulrika Jonsson: The last thing you take off before going to bed.
Contestant: Your feet.

From *Family Feud* (CBS):

Host: Give a good reason for men to dig a hole in the road.
Contestant: To dig a grave?

Host: Name a trick a dog does.
Contestant: Jump rope?

Host: Name a place where you might see a dead body.
Contestant: Your house.

Host: Name a place where you take off your clothes, besides home.
Contestant: School.

Host: Name a place you dab perfume on.
Contestant: Tip of tongue.

Host: Name a reason a man might take his toupée off.
Contestant: To show off?

Host: Name a room in the house where the family gathers.
Contestant: The bathroom.

Host: Name a Shakespeare play with a person's name in it.
Contestant: *A Midsummer Night's Dream.*

Host: Name a vegetable you marinate.
Contestant: Grapes.

Host: Name a TV show that took place on an island, past or present.
Contestant: *Miami Vice.*
Contestant 2: *General Hospital.*

Host: Name a vegetable you stuff.
Contestant: Brussels sprouts.
Contestant 2: Watermelon.

Host: Name a vegetable you've never eaten.
Contestant: Cactus.

Host: Name a product that, according to its commercials, will make you more popular.
Contestant: Toilet paper.

Host: Name an article of clothing that women buy for their husbands.
Contestant: Halter-neck top.

Host: Name an occasion when a church might have standing room only.

Contestant: New Year's Eve.

Host: Name an occupation in which people cover their faces.

Contestant: Model.

Host: Name an occupation in which you disguise your appearance.

Contestant: Doctor.

Host: Name something with a hole in it.
Contestant: Window.

> **Host:** Name something worn only by children.
> **Contestant:** Clothes.

Host: Name something you beat.
Contestant: Apple.

Host: Name something you buy by the set.
Contestant: Paper.

Host: Name something you do in the bathroom.
Contestant: Decorate.

Host: Name something you hear at a New Year's Eve party.
Contestant: Gunfire/A parade.

Host: Name something you might accidentally leave on all night.
Contestant: Shoes.

Host: Name something you would buy in a stationery store.
Contestant: Water.

Host: Name something you'd hate to discover was living in your attic.
Contestant: Furniture.

> **Host:** Name something you keep in a garden shed.
> **Contestant:** Gardener.

Host: Name something you'd see in a taxi.
Contestant: Door fittings.

Host: Name a male dancer.
Contestant: Betty Grable.

Host: Name a man's name beginning with the letter 'K'.
Contestant: Kentucky Fried Chicken.

Host: Name a bird that some people look like when they walk.
Contestant: Dolphin.

Host: Name a car known by its initials.
Contestant: Corvette.

Host: Name a cartoon character with big ears.
Contestant: Kermit the Frog.

Host: Name a city that begins with 'San'.
Contestant: Seattle.

> **Host:** Name a famous Biblical twosome.
> **Contestant:** Ralph and Susie?

Host: Name a famous woman you wouldn't want to see wearing a thong.
Contestant: Sally the Hippo?

Host: Name a food that comes in instant form.
Contestant: Asparagus.

Host: Name a food used to describe a person.
Contestant: A dog.

Host: Name a food you wish was healthy for you.
Contestant: Ketchup.

Host: Name a gift you give that comes in a bottle.
Contestant: Milk.

Host: Name a fact about Al Gore.
Contestant: He's a Republican.

Host: Name a famous Australian.
Contestant: Peter Pan.

Host: Name a holiday where stores are always busy.
Contestant: Monday.

Host: Name a household appliance you can't live without.
Contestant: Spatula.

Host: Name something in a bird cage.
Contestant: Hamster.

Host: Name a famous magician.
Contestant: Tom Cruise.

Host: Name a famous Christina.
Contestant: Christina the Car?

Host: Name something you can climb up.
Contestant: A bike.

Host: The average family size is 2.2. What is .2 of a child?
Contestant: A dog.

Host: Name a happy occasion where you feel a little let down when it's over.
Contestant: Funeral.

Host: Name an animal people fear because it's a man-eater.
Contestant: Hippo.

Host: Name something people want to be buried with.
Contestant: Their home.

Host: Name an appliance you should definitely keep your fingers out of.
Contestant: Dishwasher.

Host: Name an unwelcome gift people receive from a cat.
Contestant: A bowl.

Host: Name something that breaks out.
Contestant: A baby.

Host: Apart from 'snowman', name a word beginning with 'snow'.
Contestant: Sugar.

Host: Name something that comes in a travel size.
Contestant: Refrigerator.

Host: Name something that might be a few weeks late.
Contestant: Dying.

Host: Name something you tune.
Contestant: Fish.

Host: Name something you put under a pillow.
Contestant: Radio.

Host: How long does the average extramarital affair last?
Contestant: Three days.

Host: How long does the average honeymoon last?
Contestant: Two months.

Host: Say how often your parents punished you as a child.
Contestant: Five times.

Host: Name the person that would paint your house, if you could get somebody famous to do it.
Contestant: Mr Squiggle.

Host: Name something you think that all drivers, except you, should get a ticket for doing.
Contestant: Driving with no shoes on.

Host: Name something you wash more than once per day.
Contestant: Socks.

Host: Name something you wear two of at the same time.
Contestant: Underwear.

Host: Name a famous Kelly.
Contestant: Smelly Kelly.

NED KELLY   GRACE KELLY   SMELLY KELLY

Host: Name something that runs on a track.
Contestant: Speakers.

From *Family Fortunes* (ITV):

Les Dennis: Name something you do standing on a chair.
Contestant: Read.

Les Dennis: Name something you play in bed.
Contestant: I Spy.

Les Dennis: Name something you put out for the birds.
Contestant: Worms.

Les Dennis: Name something that comes in sevens.
Contestant: Fingers.

Les Dennis: Name something a blind man might use.
Contestant: A sword.

Les Dennis: Name something a bricklayer uses.
Contestant: Spatula.

Les Dennis: Name a high-school class people might actually enjoy going to.
Contestant: Beverly Hills.

Les Dennis: Name a domestic animal.
Contestant: Leopard.

Les Dennis: Name something that flies that doesn't have an engine.
Contestant: A bicycle with wings.

Les Dennis: Name a famous Dick.
Contestant: Carrot.

Les Dennis: Name a famous Irishman.
Contestant: Trevor McDonald.

Les Dennis: Name a famous Scotsman.
Contestant: Vinnie Jones.

Les Dennis: Name a jacket potato topping.
Contestant: Jam.

Les Dennis: Name a job a working dog does.
Contestant: Slave.

Les Dennis: Name a method of securing your home.
Contestant: Put the kettle on.

Les Dennis: Name something people believe in but cannot see.
Contestant: Hitler.

Les Dennis: Name a non-living object that has feet.
Contestant: Plant.

Les Dennis: Name a number you have to memorize.
Contestant: Seven.

Les Dennis: Name a way to toast somebody.
Contestant: Over a fire?

Les Dennis: Name something sold by gypsies.
Contestant: Bananas.

Les Dennis: Name something people have more than two of on their bodies.

Contestant: Arms.

> **Les Dennis:** Name a bird that can also be a man's name.
> **Contestant:** Chicken.

Les Dennis: Name something people play with when they are nervous.

Contestant: Violin.

Les Dennis: Name something that makes you itch.

Contestant: Fibreglass.

Les Dennis: Name a character from Cluedo.

Contestant: Steve.

Les Dennis: Name a card game that's easy to cheat at.

Contestant: Checkers.

Les Dennis: Name something you would associate with Dracula.

Contestant: Bob Monkhouse.

From *The Newlywed Game* (ABC):

Host: What is your wife's least favourite crustacean?
Contestant: Earth.

Host: What would you say is your husband's favourite form of roughage?

Contestant: I guess I'd say old newspapers …?

From *Press Your Luck* (CBS):

Peter Tomarken: On the middle row of a standard keyboard, what key should your left 'pinky' finger rest on?
Contestant: ASDF.

Peter Tomarken: What was the magical item that brought Frosty the Snowman to life?
Contestant: Corncob pipe.

From *Sale of the Century* (NBC):

Host: A compass heading of 180 indicates what direction of travel?
Contestant: Backwards.

From *Steve Wright in the Afternoon* (BBC Radio 2):

Steve Wright: On this day in 1963, how did Valentina Tereshkova become famous?
Contestant: Was she the first woman to grow a potato?

From *Today with Des and Mel* (ITV):

Melanie Sykes: You are eating a baklava. Are you having a main course or a pudding?
Contestant: A starter?

• •

From *The Sara Cox Show* (BBC Radio 1):

Sara Cox: What was Bram Stoker's most famous creation?
Contestant: Branston Pickle.

• •

From *The Weakest Link* (BBC):

Anne Robinson: A pain in the muscles or bones of the lower
legs, often suffered by sportsmen, is known as shin …?
Contestant: …dler's List?

Anne Robinson: According to the common saying, revenge is a
dish best served … cold or on toast?
Contestant: On toast.

Anne Robinson: According to the proverb, the daily consumption of what piece of fruit keeps the doctor away?

Contestant: Banana.

Anne Robinson: What 'Z' is used to describe a human who has returned from the dead?

Contestant: Unicorn.

Anne Robinson: Ken Follett is a famous what: author or photographer?

Contestant: Authotographer.

Anne Robinson: In nature, most unripe fruit is which colour: purple or green?

Contestant: Plum.

Anne Robinson: In medicine, the phrase 'contagious disease' literally means an illness that is spread by which of the five senses?

Contestant: Sight.

LOVE AND MARRIAGE

When quiz shows involve couples, it's not surprising things get out of hand. Mainly because what amuses the audience – essentially anything saucy – isn't *necessarily* the same thing that amuses your spouse, particularly when they're on the wrong end of the punchline. As you'll see from some of the entries that follow, one of the worst shows for this (or best, depending on your viewpoint), is *The Newlywed Game*, on air in the United States since 1966 and still using the phrase 'making whoopee' to mean something much ruder all these years later. Four couples, pitted against one another to find the loved-up duo who know each other best, answer questions about each other's habits and interests. At least, that's the idea.

While you can understand how, on *some* quiz shows, embarrassingly incorrect answers might provide a bonding experience (at least on *Family Fortunes* you're all making equal fools of yourselves), it's not surprising to hear that *The Newlywed Game* has allegedly been responsible for a divorce or two …

• •

From *Bingo America* (GSN):

Richard Karn: What's the price of a dozen roses?
Contestant: $1.75.

From *The Newlywed Game* (ABC):

Host: What is your favourite part of our *Newlywed Game* studio?
Contestant: Wife #2. [Not his own wife.]

Host: What is your husband's favourite thing to squeeze in the supermarket?
Contestant: His meat?

> **Host:** What is your husband's favourite thing to masticate?
> **Contestant:** The dog?

Host: 'Most of the electricity in our home flows from the ...' what to the what?
Contestant: 'From the plug to the vibrator'?

Host: What is your husband's favourite condiment?
Contestant: Um, his car?
Contestant 2: I don't know what that word means either, so I'll just say his clothes?

Host: What product name describes your romantic behaviour on your wedding night?
Contestant: The Jolly Green Giant.

Host: What word beginning with the first letter of your last name best describes your wife's chest?
Contestant: Tiny?

Host: What is your favourite amphibian?
Contestant: My wife?

Host: How long is your husband's in-seam?
Contestant: Seven inches.

Host: 'I don't know why, but my husband acts really weird whenever I try to touch …' what?
Contestant: 'His bonkers'?

Host: 'Roses are red, violets are blue, on our wedding night, our husband and I …' what?
Contestant: 'Went to bed'.

Host: Gentlemen, how long do your romantic moods usually last?
Wife: Twelve hours.
Husband: I'd be dead if that were right!

> **Host:** What was the first thing you said to your husband on your wedding night?
> **Contestant:** [thinking] Oh, gosh, that's a hard one …

Host: What gripe do you have about your husband's romantic technique?

Contestant: It's not long enough?

Host: What Spanish word would you use to describe your wife's chest?

Contestant: *Nada.*

Host: What will your husband say is the last spice or flavour you used too much of in one of your dishes?

Contestant: Burnt?

From *The Weakest Link* (NBC):

Anne Robinson: According to Hallmark, what type of gift should be given on the fiftieth wedding anniversary?

Contestant: Greeting card?

DUMB AND DUMBER
AND DUMBERERER

On some quiz shows, any old answer is preferable to none at all – which is good news for our common-senseless contestants. As quiz aficionados well know, a 'pass' on *Mastermind* is worse than a wrong answer, since it counts against you when the final scores are tallied up. It really is better to say 'turnips' than 'pass' – even if turnips are nothing to do with your specialist subject.

But as the following answers demonstrate, there are times when silence is definitely golden. And on these occasions, one cannot help wondering whether a caveman-style 'ngggh' would have been preferable to what was actually said. On TV, in public …

• •

From *Bingo America* (GSN):

Richard Karn: How many leaves are there on a four-leaf clover?
Contestant: Three.

• •

From *Bob Hope Birthday Quiz* (LBC Radio):

Host: Bob Hope was the fifth of how many sons?
Contestant: Four.

• •

From *Cash Cab* (ITV):

John Moody: Give another word for 'telltale'.
Contestant: 'Telltale'.

• •

From *Family Feud* (CBS):

Host: Name a part of the body everybody has only one of.
Contestant: Big toe.

Host: Name a part of the body with four letters.
Contestant: Arms.

Host: Name a part of the telephone.
Contestant: The bottom part.

> **Host:** Name one of the Beatles.
> **Contestant:** Lennie.

Host: Name a phrase starting with 'Father'.
Contestant: Stepfather.

Host: Name a Roman god, or the planet nearest the sun.
Contestant: Pluto/The moon/Mars/Saturn.

Host: Name a street name that is common to cities all over the US.
Contestant: Hollywood Boulevard.

Host: Name a TV show with the word 'family' in the title.
Contestant: *The Generation Game.*

Host: Name a state with good skiing.
Contestant: Florida.

Host: Name something a duck and a chicken have in common.
Contestant: They quack.

> **Host:** Name something you'd find in an operating room.
> **Contestant:** Operator.

Host: Name something associated with a typical surfer.
Contestant: The sea.

Host: Name something most people have only one of.
Contestant: Grandparents.

Host: Name something you do in the event of a power cut.
Contestant: Switch the light on.

Host: Name something you do while you sunbathe.
Contestant: Lay in the sun.

Host: Name something you learn how to do from a how-to book.
Contestant: Read.

Host: Name something you might find in a manicure set.
Contestant: A wig.

Host: Name something you might find on an old pirate ship, besides pirates.
Contestant: A wrecked pirate ship.

Host: Name something your car has two of.
Contestant: Wheels.

Host: The month of pregnancy where a woman begins to look pregnant.
Contestant: September.

Host: Name a bill that's always more than you expected it to be.
Contestant: A hundred-dollar bill/A fifty-dollar bill.

Host: Name a beverage you stir before drinking.
Contestant: Water.

Host: Name an age when you are neither young nor old?
Contestant: Twenty.

Host: Name something you often misplace in your car.
Contestant: Steering wheel.

Host: Name a yellow fruit.
Contestant: Orange.

Host: Name something Russia is famous for.
Contestant: Russians/Wheat.

Host: The heaviest item in your house.
Contestant: 600 pounds.

Host: The one word people yell to their dog.
Contestant: 'Here, boy!'

Host: The one word that people yell at the end of a performance.
Contestant: 'I love you.'

Host: Name something starting with 'egg'.
Contestant: Excellent/Eggland.

Host: Name something starting with the word 'Club'.
Contestant: Golf club.

Host: Name something that comes with a summer storm.
Contestant: Snow.

From *Family Fortunes* (ITV):

Les Dennis: Name a part of the body beginning with the letter 'N'.

Contestant: Knee.

Les Dennis: Name a word that rhymes with 'money'?

Contestant: 'Money'.

Andy Collins: Name a famous historical heroine.

Contestant: Winston Churchill.

Les Dennis: Name a Cluedo character.
Contestant: Dr Morse.

> **Les Dennis:** Name something that floats in a bath?
> **Contestant:** Water.

Les Dennis: Name a bird with a long neck.
Contestant: Blackbird.

Les Dennis: Name a bird with long legs.
Contestant: Sparrow.

Les Dennis: Name a bird with long legs.
Contestant: Turkey.

> **Les Dennis:** Name something red.
> **Contestant:** My cardigan.

Les Dennis: Name a boy's name beginning with 'J'.
Contestant: Gerald.

Les Dennis: Name a cheese named after an English county.
Contestant: Philadelphia.

From *Fifteen to One* (Channel 4):

William G. Stewart: From the NATO phonetic alphabet, 'Papa, Quebec, Romeo …' What comes next?
Contestant: 'Delta'.

• •

From *Fort Boyard* (Challenge TV):

Jodie Penfold: Arrange these two groups of letters to form a
word: 'CHED' and 'PIT'.
Contestant: Chedpit?

• •

From *Judgemental* (BBC One):

Sophie Raworth: The category is 'Birds'. When a person has no
hair, they are said to be 'as bald as a …' what?
Contestant: 'Chicken'.

• •

From *Lorraine Kelly Today* (ITV):

Lorraine Kelly: How many days in a leap year?
Contestant: 253.

• •

From *The Owen Money Show* (BBC Radio Wales):

Owen Money: In thirty seconds, name as many well-known
politicians as you can.
Contestant: Err … Tony Brown … and Nigel Benn. [Silence.]

• •

From *Press Your Luck* (CBS):

Peter Tomarken: In which of the three daily meals are you most
likely to eat fatty foods?
Contestant: Meat.

From *Sale of the Century* (ITV):

Host: How many 'R's are there in 'irreversible'?
Contestant: Twelve.

From *See Hear Saturday* (BBC):

Lara Crooks: What is the most abundant gas in the
    atmosphere?
Contestant: Air.

From *This Morning with Richard and Judy* (ITV):

John Leslie: At what time is *Midday Money* broadcast?
Contestant: 12.15.

From *The Weakest Link* (BBC):

Anne Robinson: How many 'E's are there in 'argument'?
Contestant: Three.

Anne Robinson: How many 'L's are there in 'intelligent'?
Contestant: One.

Anne Robinson: In management, which 'P' is the term used for
    getting a higher-ranked job and often a pay rise?
Contestant: Don't know.

Anne Robinson: In spelling, what consonant is found in both
    'good' and 'bad'?
Contestant: 'O'.

Anne Robinson: In olden times, what were minstrels: travelling entertainers or chocolate salesmen?

Contestant: Chocolate salesmen.

Anne Robinson: What four-letter word beginning with 'D' has shelves and is used for writing on?

Contestant: Table.

Anne Robinson: What 'D' is a large city in the Republic of Ireland?

Contestant: Belfast.

Anne Robinson: What is the more common name given to the government department Military Intelligence Six?

Contestant: MI5.

Anne Robinson: What kind of dozen is thirteen?

Contestant: Half a dozen.

Anne Robinson: What sign of the Zodiac is represented by a fish?

Contestant: The Zodiac.

Anne Robinson: Which letter comes between 'P' and 'R'?

Contestant: 'O'.

Anne Robinson: 'Bolster' is an anagram of which marine crustacean?

Contestant: Crab.

Anne Robinson: Introduced in Britain in 1978, the State Earnings Related Pension Scheme is better known by what acronym?

Contestant: PAYE.

Anne Robinson: Single combat is a fight between how many people?

Contestant: One person.

AND FINALLY …
A TURKEY

Though the disciples of dimness in this book are genuinely – and rather worryingly – actual, real-life people who exist in the actual, real-life world, what follows is so very silly, you almost can't believe the contestant really is of this earth.

It's the mid-eighties and Bob Johnson, a gentleman of advancing years, giggly demeanour and silver hair, is representing his relatives on the final 'Big Money' round of *Family Fortunes*. Max Bygraves is hosting, the lights are dimmed and the huge, dot-matrix, black and yellow board shines brightly. It gradually becomes quite clear that, panicked beyond measure beneath the studio lights, poor old Bob is nervous; there is only one word in his head. And that word is 'turkey'.

• •

Max Bygraves: Name something people take with them to the beach.
Contestant: Turkey?

[0 points awarded]

Max Bygraves: The first thing you'd buy in the supermarket.
Contestant: Turkey?

[0 points awarded]

Max Bygraves: A food often stuffed.
Contestant: Turkey!

[21 points awarded]

· ·

As it turned out, there was a genuine reason for his strange obsession with the Christmas bird. Having overheard the answer 'chicken' while in the isolation booth (they hadn't fitted his headphones correctly), Bob decided 'turkey' must be worth a try for one of the five final questions. Quite how he thought he might win by answering 'turkey' for three of the five questions remains a mystery. Needless to say, the Johnsons went home empty-handed.

ACKNOWLEDGEMENTS

Fifteen bonus points to Hannah Knowles and Lynsey Sutherland for pressing their buzzers on the original idea for this book. Which would not have been written by *me* had the following people not been completely wondair: Mum and Dad (thank you from the bottom of my silly old heart, for all you do), Sarah (who writes with a scalpel) and lastly John and Jem (cleverness and charm *are* hereditary, then).

Hearty thanks also go to Kay Hayden (for the delightful design), Andrew Pinder (charming illustrations) and Sarah Sandland (perkily enthusiastic publicity). It should go without saying that everyone mentioned here deserves a nice, wet snog from a sexily angry Paxman. Or a speedboat. You know, whichever you prefer.

· ·